Big
Business
Economic Power in a Free Society

Big
Business
Economic Power in a Free Society

Advisory Editor
LEON STEIN

Editorial Board
Stuart Bruchey
Thomas C. Cochran

A NOTE ABOUT THIS BOOK

A careful and scholarly study of the talents that enabled men like Astor, Gould, Rockefeller and Morgan to accumulate their great fortunes. Did their acquisitive efficiency reflect unique character traits, family heritage, special community service, diluted ethical imperatives, shrewdness or the ability to foretell the future? The book traces the rise of individual family fortunes in the days before corporate anonymity.

The Economic Causes
of Great Fortunes

BY

Anna Youngman

ARNO PRESS
A New York Times Company
New York / 1973

Reprint Edition 1973 by Arno Press Inc.

Reprinted from a copy in The Newark Public Library

BIG BUSINESS: Economic Power in a Free Society
ISBN for complete set; 0-405-05070-4
See last pages of this volume for titles.

Manufactured in the United States of America

————◆————

Library of Congress Cataloging in Publication Data

Youngman, Anna Prichitt.
    The economic causes of great fortunes. *75-089*

    (Big business: economic power in a free society)
    Reprint of the ed. published by Bankers Pub. Co.,
New York.
    Originally presented as the author's thesis, Univer-
sity of Chicago, 1909.
    1. Wealth--United States.   2. United States--
Economic conditions.   I. Title.   II. Series.
HB821.Y82 1973   330.1'6   73-2543
ISBN 0-405-05121-2

The Economic Causes of Great Fortunes

BY

Anna Youngman, Ph. D.

NEW YORK
THE BANKERS PUBLISHING CO.
1909

CONTENTS.

CHAPTER I.

INTRODUCTION.

AN examination of the causes of great fortunes may be undertaken in either one of two ways. The analysis may be (1) impersonally theoretical, seeking only occasional corroboration by an appeal to the facts, or it may be based (2) upon a detailed examination of particular fortunes, conclusions being strictly deduced from a consideration of the facts presented.

The first method of procedure is apt to give rise to grave errors. Mistakes are likely to occur frequently, because of a failure to recognize the operation of certain factors, which, in the absence of a detailed study, are either unknown or else appear unworthy of notice. Furthermore, a theoretical analysis which makes an appeal to the facts for confirmation, instead of being based, in the first place, upon the facts furnished by a specific inquiry, presupposes an *à priori* judgment of what aspects of the question under discussion are worthy of consideration. This judgment once formed, the facts are apt to be coerced, however unconsciously, to support the position taken.

The second method of investigation is conceived to be the more legitimate, although it has some obvious limitations. The most patent objection is, of course, the difficulty of disentangling from a heterogeneous mass of material only such facts as appear to be of a causally relevant nature. There is always a danger that undue emphasis may be given to circumstances, which, although important in the single instance, have less significance for the general question bearing on the causes of the growth of large fortunes. However, by examining in detail a number of fortunes differing in respect to the time and the manner of acquisition, and by subsequently subjecting them to an unbiased analysis, any general results that may be deduced will have a degree of validity unattainable by the more impersonal method. In brief, a basis for theorizing will be afforded, which will be sound, just in so far as the preceding studies have been accurate, exhaustive, and well selected.

It must, of course, be conceded that the question of selection calls for the exercise of considerable judgment; and if the fortunes examined do not represent sufficiently diverse types of activity, then the facts are likely to support a distorted theoretical conclusion of but limited application. The fortunes which have been selected for examination in the following study, although few in number, represent a highly diversified range of economic activity, and they cover a period sufficiently lengthy to include the several phases of commercial and industrial development through which the United States has passed since the Revolutionary War.

The fortune of John Jacob Astor, gained from trade and from land-speculations, is the typical American fortune of the pre-corporate *régime.*[1] The Gould fortune is a product of the period that intervened between the close of Astor's career and the distinctively industrial era of the present day. It was made chiefly by means of speculative investments in the securities of various railroads, and it is one of a number of fortunes similarly acquired, at a time when the railroads of the country were practically the only great public-service corporations in existence. It is not only representative of its time, however, but it offers certain unique and picturesque features incident to "high finance," which call for explanation in any study of great fortunes. Finally, the fortunes of the "Standard Oil" and the "Morgan" men, although originating generally

---

[1]To be sure, Astor's Fur Company was incorporated, but merely as a matter of form, since Astor owned the business entirely, with the exception of a few shares granted to his subordinates.

at an earlier period, present all the characteristics of the modern situation, in which industrial
corporations vie with the railroads in their importance for purposes of speculation and of
investment.

In the days of John Jacob Astor, the growth
of a great fortune could be studied in isolation,
and the activities of its owner could be narrated
almost without reference to the existence of his
contemporaries. With the exception of certain
subordinates to whom he granted a minor interest, Astor did not have even a partner in his
great fur company. As for his real-estate investments, he would have been exceedingly loath
to share with another the immense gains which
came to him from that source. But even in the
time of Jay Gould there had come about a
change. Gould, individualist though he was,
made his fortune under a corporate *régime,* and
he was thereby compelled to identify himself
more or less with those interested in the same
corporate undertakings. To understand fully
the activities of Gould, one must, for example,
know somewhat of the career of James Fisk; and
for a complete knowledge of Gould's later undertakings, it is essential to remember that he was
supported by a small coterie of men, most of
whom were directors of the Union Pacific at the

time of his entry into that road. However, his interests and those of his associates were confined almost exclusively to one field—railroads. It is not necessary to seek for ramifications of his interests into other fields, through the mediation of these lesser members of the group. It becomes possible, therefore, to gauge the extent of his wealth and influence, and to analyze the causes making for his personal gain, by a simple examination of his individual operations.

But of late years conditions have changed. As a result of the interrelations made possible under a highly-developed corporate system of business enterprise, the man of great fortune has come more and more to be regarded as but a member of a group of men having great fortunes. It is less than a quarter of a century since the idea of a group activity began to secure recognition; but today it has become possible to speak familiarly of the "Standard Oil" or of the "Morgan" men. More than that, the group has attained such importance that, to understand the nature and sources of an individual's gain, it is necessary to undertake an examination of the character and the activities of the group of which he is a member. It is still possible, of course, to trace the history of the way in which Mr. Rockefeller, for example, laid the foundation of his fortune in

the Standard Oil Company (although that has
been done *ad nauseam*). But Mr. Rockefeller's
Standard Oil holdings are but a part of the numerous interests in which he, as a member of the
so-called "Standard Oil" group, shares. It is,
in fact, through group activity that he and many
others, who are counted among the richest men
of the country, are today enlarging their private
fortunes, and the group should, therefore, receive consideration in any study attempting to
explain the causes of the accumulations of men
of great fortune. For that reason, it is proposed
to treat the fortunes of the men of today from the
standpoint of the group, rather than that of the
individual, while the fortunes of John Jacob
Astor and Jay Gould will be used to illustrate
the individualistic methods of acquisition.

CHAPTER II.

THE FORTUNE OF JOHN JACOB ASTOR.[1]

I.

WHEN John Jacob Astor landed in America in the spring of 1784, he encountered a civilization industrially unique and wholly alien to his brief experience. Witness the anecdote that is told concerning his astonishment at being able to secure a position unhampered by the payments and regulations of apprenticeship.[2] The lack of social restraints upon the freedom of production and exchange seemed, no doubt, peculiarly inviting to one who must have imbibed, even if

---

[1] John Jacob Astor was born in Waldorf, Germany, in 1763, the son of a butcher. At the age of sixteen or seventeen he left home, working his way to the coast, whence he took ship for Engand. After four years spent in London with a firm of flute- and piano-makers, of which his brother was a member, he set sail for America, having accumulated money enough to pay for a passage in the steerage and to provide himself with a few additional pounds sterling.

For incidents of his early life cf. James Parton, *Life of Astor,* New York, 1865; Washington Irving, *Astoria;* J. D. McCabe, *Great Fortunes and How They Were Made,* 1871; *Hunt's Merchants' Magazine,* Vol XI, p. 153; W. O. Stoddard, *Men of Achievement,* 1901; W. W. Astor, *Pall Mall,* Vol. XVIII.

[2] Parton's *Life of Astor* (New York), 1865.

unconsciously, old-world ideas of privilege. Add
to this that the country held numberless untested
possibilities of wealth development, and it is not
hard to predicate the pecuniary success of an
individual such as John Jacob Astor, who could
boast a more than ordinary amount of commercial astuteness.

It is not to be inferred, however, that the
country was in all respects industrially unex-
ploited, nor that the fur trade and foreign shipping, the fields in which Astor was to lay the
foundations of his fortune, were absolutely un-
tried.   Indeed, the fur-bearing regions of the
continent had been tramped over long ere this by
adventurous employees of the early French companies, by trained agents of the Hudson's Bay
Company, and by resolute traders and trappers
who were independent of all organized ventures.
Moreover, before the war of the Revolution, the
natural products of the colonies had given rise
to a lucrative carrying-trade which showed indications of a speedy revival after the Peace of
Paris under the direction of Boston merchants
of considerable wealth.[3]   But after all, the exploitation of these two fields of commercial ac-

---

[3]Weeden, *Economic and Social History of New England,* Vol.
II, p. 821; cf. also MacPherson, *On Commerce,* Vol. IV, pp. 57,
117, 195.

tivity was only in its initial stages. In 1784, New York was as yet of secondary importance as a center of the American foreign trade, while the condition of the fur-trade is evidenced by the fact that the western part of New York state and even portions of Long Island were still prolific of peltries.

That John Jacob Astor at the age of twenty should have come in contact with a loquacious countryman who impressed upon him the money-getting possibilities of the fur-trade, was a piece of rare good luck.[4] The elements of fortune—even for the wholly penniless—were all there, though no doubt it required a laudable effort of the imagination for a young man so entirely ignorant of the conditions prevailing in America to appraise them at their full value. To begin with, the fur-trader required only a minimum capital; as Astor's German acquaintance told him, with a basket of toys or even cakes, valuable furs could be bought on the wharves and in the markets of New York, which could be sold with advantage to resident merchants, or, if sent to London, disposed of at an advance of 400 or 500 per cent.[5]

---

[4] Cf. references previously given to "Lives" of Astor.

[5] Parton, *Life of John Jacob Astor* (New York, 1865). Parton is unreliable, but the statement seems probable in the light of other evidence concerning the profits of the fur-trade.

Such extraordinary returns are the natural result of trading operations carried on between two civilizations having entirely different standards of value. Both civilizations may conceivably profit by these operations, but the greater part of the gain is very likely to accrue to one of them at the expense of the other. In the case of the white men and the Indians of North America, the gains arising from commercial intercourse were confined almost exclusively to the former, though, it must be confessed, their pecuniary successes were often attended with severe personal hardship and occasional loss of life. At its inception the Indian trade was but slightly influenced by a trade-morality even of the mildest sort, so that the ignorance of the Indian combined with his susceptibility to drink and finery delivered him over to the greater or less cupidity of the white man. An idea may be had of the conditions confronting fur-traders in the remote comparatively unworked regions of the country by consulting some of the schedules preserved by pioneers in the field.[6] It is quite evident from these schedules that there must have been an opportunity for great profits in such exchanges.

[6]Alexander Henry, who began his career as a fur-trader in 1760, has left an account of his travels and adventures, in which he has embodied a list of the prices of goods bought from the Indians at Fort des Prairies:

Indeed, the fact is patent, even though various
incidental expenses connected with obtaining the
skins and transporting them to market are not

```
A gun........................20 beaver skins
A stroud blanket.............10   "      "
A white blanket.............. 8   "      "
An ax (1 lb.)................ 3   "      "
½ pt. gunpowder............ 1   "      "
10 balls..................... 1   "      "
```

The principal profits, however, he says, came from the sale of
knives, beads, flints, steels, awls, and other small articles. Tobacco, for which the Indians showed a decided preference, sold
at the rate of one foot of Spencer's twist (a twist of black
tobacco about an inch in diameter) for each beaver skin, while
rum was dispensed at the rate of two beaver skins per bottle.
Penny prints, such as are sold to children, were considered
especially valuable as talismans, and Henry states that they
were an exceedingly fertile source of profit, although he gives no
exact information as to rates of exchange. (Alexander Henry,
Travels and Adventures in Canada and the Indian Territories,
ed. by James Bain [new ed., 1901], p. 320.) Bain thinks Astor
conducted his trade in furs at Montreal under Henry's direction.
    Russell gives a schedule of the trade of the Hudson's Bay Co.
in 1788.

```
A common musket..............10 beaver skins
A pound of powder............ 2   "      "
4 pounds of shot.............. 1   "      "
A hatchet .................... 1   "      "
6 knives  .................... 1   "      "
A pound of glass beads........ 2   "      "
A cloth coat.................. 6   "      "
A petticoat  ................. 5   "      "
A pound of snuff.............. 1   "      "
```

Combs, looking-glasses, brandy, and other articles were exchanged in proportion, Russell states rather indefinitely. Moreover, in the exchange two otter skins and three martens were
reckoned the equivalent of one beaver skin, whereas a single fine
skin of either otter or marten was worth more than a beaver.
Bancroft, *History of the Northwest Coast,* Vol. I, p. 459, quotes
the statements of Russell made in his *History of America,* Vol.
II, p. 263.

2

estimated, while the prices at which they were eventually sold are not stated. However, some definite testimony on this head is afforded by Alexander Ross who, while connected with the Astorian venture, spent a winter in the interior (600 miles from the mouth of the Columbia River), in a region not previously invaded by trade. During the 188 days of his stay he procured 1,550 beavers, besides other peltries estimated to be worth £2,250 in Canton, which averaged the company 5½d. each, or £35 sterling in all. Ross says:

So anxious were they [i. e., the Indians] to trade and so fond of tobacco that one morning before breakfast I obtained 110 skins for leaf tobacco at the rate of five leaves per skin, and at last when I had but one yard of white cotton remaining one of the chiefs gave me 29 prime beaver skins for it.[7]

Enough has been said, perhaps, to illustrate the enormous profits arising out of such transactions with the Indians, although it must be remembered that losses due to accidents in transport, Indian uprisings, and other unforeseen happenings had to be taken into account, while the salaries of subordinates, and the maintenance of trading-posts were items of large expense to the organized companies.

[7] Alexander Ross, *Adventures of the First Settlers on the Oregon or Columbia River*, 1810-13. Reprint by Thwaites of the London edition of 1849, p. 158; *Early Western Travels*, edited by Reuben Gold Thwaites, Vol. VII, 1904.

This, then, was the trade to which John Jacob Astor addressed himself upon his arrival in America. He engaged his services to a New York dealer who bought and exported peltries, and soon he was making trips to Montreal in the interests of his employer, gathering information as to the possibilities of the trade, and acquiring adroitness in dealing with the natives. The accounts concerning this early period of Astor's life are meager, conflicting in details, and prone to substitute eulogy for facts. But it would probably be safe to say that by 1786 or thereabouts he had severed his connection with Mr. Bowne, his employer, and with a small stock in trade had established an independent business. He obtained his furs, apparently, not only from the Indians themselves, but from white trappers and from the occupants of farm-houses throughout New York state.[8]

The actual expenses of such a trade were of course slight, and if connections could but be established with those markets where furs were in greatest demand, profits might rise to many times the original outlay. That John Jacob Astor should have thought of London as the goal of his operations—the market in which he

---

[8] Parton, *Life of Astor;* also, cf. other accounts of Astor's l'f, that have been cited.

could take advantage of the largest price discrepancies—is not altogether surprising, especially
since the merchants of Montreal with whom he
had come in contact all shipped their furs to
London.[9] Nevertheless, the energy and dispatch
with which he put his plans into execution were
indicative of a quite extraordinary enterprise.
Very early in his career,[10] in fact, as soon as he
had accumulated a sufficiently large stock of furs,
and had saved money enough to pay for a passage in the steerage, he set out for London with
the purpose of forming connections there which
would permit him to avail himself of the high
prices of a European center of distribution. Evidently this venture was successful (though no
direct information on the subject is to be got)
for Astor's profits grew steadily until by 1794[11]
he was in a position to devolve all but the man-
agerial and financial work connected with his undertakings upon subordinates.[12]

---

[9]Indeed, the furs obtained in Montreal must perforce be
shipped to London, as there was a law against exporting them
from British possessions; cf. George Bryce, *The Remarkable
History of the Hudson's Bay Co.*, p. 192 (Toronto, 1900).

[10]As to the exact time accounts are conflicting and extremely
unreliable.

[11]In 1794 Jay's Treaty resulted in the relinquishment of the
trading-posts held by the British within the territory of the United
States.

[12]"In a dozen years [he] had diverted some of the most
profitable markets from his competitors and was at the head of

About this time he bought a vessel of his own in which to ship his furs to London. There, it is said, he heard of the trade of the East India Company with China, and, in consequence, in 1800 sent his first ship to Canton.[13] Whether or no he had to go so far afield to learn the lucrative nature of the China trade, may well be matter for debate. An enterprising merchant and shipper who had acquired a fair-sized working capital would have been very likely at that period, when considering the advisability of extending his trade, to have looked toward Canton, especially if he dealt in a commodity such as furs, which found an eager and extensive market in China.

Weeden, discussing the revival of trade after peace had destroyed the profitable occupation of privateering, says:

In 1783 they· had begun to agitate the China trade in Salem. In 1784 the Connecticut men mooted the same question and asked for state aid in so large a venture, which the sturdy farmers in the legislature wisely declined. In the same year Captain John Green sailed direct in the ship Empress from New York for Canton. In 1785 Elias Hasket Derby cleared his ship Grand

a business branching to Albany, Buffalo, Plattsburg, and Detroit." Cf. article on *John Jacob Astor* by William Waldorf Astor, *Pall Mall,* Vol. XVIII, p. 171.

13Parton, *Life of John Jacob Astor* (New York, 1865); also *Pall Mall,* Vol. XVIII. William Waldorf Astor writes that "before the end of the century he had, to quote his own expression, 'a million dollars afloat,' which represented a fleet of a dozen vessels."

Turk, Captain West, from Salem for the Isle of France, and finally for Canton.[14]

Thomas H. Perkins, who had been trained by Derby, also became prominent in the China trade, his vessels going chiefly to the northwest coast of America and from there to China and Boston. For over fifty years (from 1792 onwards) he was engaged in this trade, and it was claimed that in the early nineteenth century no private firm in the world transacted more business in the China trade.[15] Weeden says again:

> Like all grand commerce of the olden time, the China trade was a mighty round of small exchanges multiplied into the final freight of rich goods which included all the accumulated values that had gone before.[16]

Ginseng and specie were particularly in demand for the outward bound cargoes, while the ships came back laden with tea, coffee, muslins, silks, and other fine fabrics. The customary profits on muslins and calicoes from Calcutta in those early days were estimated at 100 per cent. and over.[17]

---

[14]Weeden, *Economic and Social History of New England,* Vol. II, pp. 820, 821; cf. also MacPherson, *On Commerce,* Vol. IV, p. 57.

[15]Weeden, *Economic and Social History of New England,* Vol. II, p. 822.

[16]*Ibid.,* Vol. II, p. 824.

[17]In 1789 four of Derby's ships were in Canton, and he recorded (1785-99) 125 voyages, 45 of which were either to India or to China.

It is not surprising that the foreign carrying-trade should have taken this particular direction. No doubt enterprising American merchantmen would have engaged in it even before the Revolutionary War, had not the East India Company held a monopoly of the China trade. The goods imported into China were there exchanged for other goods which, brought back to Europe or to America, yielded a very handsome profit that offered decided inducements to a shipper wishing to extend his operations. The "Empress of China," for instance, on her pioneer voyage to Canton in February, 1784, loaded chiefly with ginseng, obtained a return cargo whose sale netted a profit estimated at $30,000—a sum exceeding 25 per cent. of the capital employed.[18] As in the Indian trade, profits grew out of an exchange between widely separated peoples of different degrees of civilization and of diverse tastes. However, the resemblance probably goes no further, as the Chinese merchant was, no doubt, as

---

In this year, 1789, fifteen American vessels entered the port of Canton; cf. MacPherson, *On Commerce*, Vol. IV, p. 195.

In 1788 a Boston ship-master began to obtain furs from the Indians of the northwest coast which were carried to Canton and exchanged for Chinese produce. From 1799 to 1818, 108 American vessels were engaged in this trade, 15,000 sea-otter skins being collected and carried to Canton in 1802. (Bancroft, *History of the Northwest Coast,* Vol. I, p. 359.)

[18]"Life of Major Samuel Shaw, First Consul at Canton," *Hunt's Merchants' Magazine,* Vol. XVIII.

astute as the Yankee trader, though the latter
could not fail to profit by the enhanced values
of his importations, resulting from the creation of
certain place utilities.   The goods shipped to
China, natural products such as furs, ginseng,
and quicksilver, [19] were exported from a country
with a relatively small population, having a relatively slight demand for such commodities, to a
densely populated district, where the peculiar
tastes of the inhabitants afforded an eager market for them.   Moreover, they came from a virgin country to a region whose natural resources
had been thoroughly exploited, a circumstance
which likewise tended greatly to enhance price
discrepancies.   In addition, the American trader
profited by the introduction into his own country
of the teas, silks, and fine fabrics of China for
which there was an ever-growing demand with
the increase of wealth and the development of
luxurious tastes.   He was also advantaged by
the fact that China had practically a monopoly
of all such commodities, so that the supply imported could to a certain extent be regulated to
meet changes in demand.

There is no available information concerning
the exact nature and extent of Astor's Chinese

---

[19]Sandalwood also, obtained in the Sandwich Islands, was imported by American shippers.

ventures. It must suffice that he sent quantities of furs to Canton, and brought back chests of tea in exchange. His tea ships were evidently the source of considerable profits, as it is said that his loss of over a million [20] in the Astorian venture was more than compensated by the profits from his tea, which arrived safely despite the war with Great Britain.[21] Another circumstance that contrived to render the import trade profitable was the method of payment of imposts.[22]

---

[20]Stated by Parton. William Waldorf Astor estimates his losses at $800,000.

[21]A table showing the imports of tea from China during a series of years will enable one to form an idea of the exceptional gains to be derived by a merchant with tea to sell in the years 1810-15.

IMPORTS OF TEA (IN POUNDS)

	Millions		Millions
1804-5	7.6	1810-11	2.6
1805-6	9.8	1811-12	3.4
1806-7	9.4	1812-13	1.4
1807-8	5.6	1813-15	1.4
1808-9	1.5	1815-16	7.7
1809-10	9.2	1816-17	9.3

[22]McCabe, *Great Fortunes and How They Were Made* (1871), p. 77; also, *Life of Moses Taylor, Hunt's Merchants' Magazine,* June, 1864, contains an incidental reference to the favorable effects of the prevailing system of government credits.

The American State Papers, Finance, Vol. V, p. 277, give some statistics concerning the amount of the duties on tea which are as follows:

	1801-12	1812-17	1817-24
Bohea	12c	24c	12c
Imperial gunpowder	...	50c	...
Hyson	32c	64c	40c

A letter from a Boston merchant dated December, 1825 (cf. *American State Papers, Finance,* Vol. V. pp. 279, 280) also gives

The United States allowed nine, twelve, and in some cases eighteen months to elapse before the payment was demanded, and in the meantime the goods brought in could be sold at an advance over cost plus duties, and with the proceeds other ships could be sent to Canton and return before the duty-bonds were due. In this way, says McCabe, John Jacob Astor had free of interest from the government during a period of eighteen or twenty years over $5,000,000. The statement seems not improbable if it be remembered that the duties on tea were very high, and that they were increased in some cases 100 per cent. for the years 1812-17, as a result of the war. During this time, it should be borne in mind, John Jacob Astor is said to have been exceptionally fortunate in bringing in his ships.

McCabe[23] quotes Francis in his *Old Merchants*

---

valuable information concerning the schedule of duties and the relation of these to cost. "It so happens," he says, "that I can give you facts in place of speculation in answer to your inquiry as to the cost of tea in China. Within a week two of our ships have come direct from Canton." Imperial gunpowder, costing 42 cents per pound, pays a duty of 50 cents; Hyson, costing 37 cents, pays a duty of 40 cents; Souchong, costing 15½ cents, pays a duty of 25 cents; while Congo pays a duty equal to about 170 per cent. of its cost. "The teas usually bought," writes the merchant, "cost us about 40 cents or 32 cents per pound and pay a duty of 40 cents." Since the percentage of duties to cost was in general considerably larger than this during the war period, the immense advantage to be obtained from deferring the payment of such duties is obvious.

[23] McCabe, *Great Fortunes and How They Were Made* (1871), pp. 76, 77.

of New York because of a specific instance given by the latter of the way in which dilatory governmental regulations operated to the gain of the merchants. The illustration is suggestive, however hypothetical the statistics may be. The Griswolds, owning the ship "Panama," start from New York with a cargo worth $200,000, $30,000 of which is invested in ginseng, spelter, lead, iron, etc., while the remainder consists of 170,000 Spanish dollars. The ship lands at Canton and returns with a cargo of tea in exchange for the commodities carried thither. The tea upon importation pays a duty equal to twice its estimated value. If the cargo brought in is assumed to be worth $200,000, it will therefore pay a duty of $400,000, and will thereafter be valued at $600,000. Estimating that the profits from the sale of the tea will be fifty per cent. of the original cost of $200,000, the cargo then becomes worth $700,000. The tea will probably be sold to wholesale grocers soon after its arrival, the purchasers giving their notes due at the end of four or six months. These notes may be discounted by the shippers, and with the proceeds two more vessels with a cargo of $200,000 each may be sent to Canton, and return before the $400,000 debt due to the government has to be paid.

No doubt this is a somewhat exaggerated statement of the case, and it has further to be considered that decided dangers lurked in the system of deferred payments. It might, for instance, impel a too venturesome merchant to import excessive quantities of tea, thus flooding the market and depressing prices, with the result that his sales would not bring in a sufficient sum to enable him to pay his indebtedness to the government, and he would consequently be forced into bankruptcy. Indeed, there are to be found occasional unsubstantiated references to attempts of John Jacob Astor to steady the market by buying up excess supplies of tea. He, no doubt, enjoyed the advantage of being able to carry his tea indefinitely, and thereby escaped in part the evils of price fluctuations. Very likely he may have profited by the facilities for purchase afforded by low prices just as wealthy would-be investors to-day profit in times of panic by obtaining bargains in securities. On the other hand, the merchants who were forced to sell in order to meet their payments were put in a position similar to that of speculators, who in case of financial stress must sacrifice their holdings to meet current obligations. However, there is but little basis in fact for the conjectures that have been advanced concerning Astor's operations in tea.

It would merely seem from hints thrown out here and there that he must have pursued some such plan, although just how far he was enabled to influence the market at large by his operations, it is impossible to state.

But John Jacob Astor enjoyed an advantage other than the ones inherent in the trade itself. He had not to play the part of an ordinary buyer in the acquisition of goods for his outward-bound cargoes, at least in so far as those cargoes were composed of furs. His final profits were a compound of the profits of the fur-trader and the shipper of furs. The extent of the profits of the fur-trader have been suggested, at any rate, by certain schedules that have been previously stated. Even allowing for the additional expenses that came with an extensive and more elaborate corporate form of organization, profits were still excessive.[24] Moreover, there were even

---

[24]The following statistics were compiled by an Indian agent for the years 1815-30, at a time when furs had become scarcer and Indians more sophisticated.

THE FUR TRADE ON THE MISSOURI AND ITS WATERS INCLUDING THE ROCKY MOUNTAINS.

Expenditures.

20 clerks, 15 yrs., at $500.............................	$ 150,000
200 men, 15 yrs., at 150.............................	450,000
Merchandise	1,500,000
Total	$2,100,000

greater returns to be got by that trader who could send his skins directly to the principal European markets. John Jacob Astor, we are told, had established commercial relations with many parts of the world as early as 1800. What must then have been his profits a decade later, after he had organized the American Fur Company which was operating in a comparatively virgin field and yet was having its furs shipped to the foremost distributive centers?

Until the time that the American Fur Company was chartered Astor had conducted his business without recourse to a formal organization of any sort, but as he pushed his operations farther west into the region of the Great Lakes, and met with the opposition of British corpora-

---

24—Continued. *Returns.*

26,000 buffalo skins per yr. 15 yrs., at $3............	$1,170,000
25,000 lbs. beaver skin per year 15 yrs., at $4 per lb...	1,500,000
4,000 otter skins per yr. 15 yrs., at $3.............	180,000
12,000 coon skins per yr. 15 yrs., at 25c.............	45,000
150,000 lbs. deer skin per yr. 15 yrs., at 33c per lb....	742,500
37,500 muskrat skins per yr. 15 yrs., at 20c.........	112,500
Total	$3,750,000
Profits	1,650,000
Average annual expenditure........................	$140,000
Average annual returns............................	250,000
Average annual profits............................	110,000

—*Senate Document No. 90, Twenty-second Congress, First Session,* p. 53.

The statistics are apparently general estimates, not compiled with reference to any particular company.

tions, he evidently decided to give his business a more definite form.   In 1808, therefore, he applied for a charter from the state of New York for the American Fur Company (capital $1,000,000)—a general title designed to include all his operations.[25]   The Mackinaw Company, a British concern which held the trade about the upper lakes and westward to the Mississippi, was a formidable competitor, but Astor in conjunction with certain members of the North West Company bought it out (1811), and organized a new association, the South West Company, which included the British organization and the American Fur Company.   Astor was to have a two-thirds interest in the trade of the United States with the understanding that all of it was to be his at the end of five years.   However, this arrangement was never put into execution, because shortly thereafter the War of 1812 broke out,[26] and the fur-trade lapsed into a state of demoralization for the time being.

Meantime Astor was putting to the test a masterly scheme of commercial enterprise, daring but

[25]*Michigan Pioneer Collections.*   Vol. XI, p. 189; *Pall Mall,* Vol. XVIII, p. 184; H. M. Chittenden, *History of the American Fur Trade of the Far West,* Vol. I, p. 167.

[26]*History of the American Fur Trade of the Far West,* Vol. I, p. 310; Bancroft, *History of the Northwest Coast,* Vol. I, p. 512.

plausible, requiring large expenditures but promising extravagant returns.   It was a scheme, in
short, that could be attempted only by a man of
large resources who could afford to wait years
for his investment to repay the original outlay.
The Astorian plan was a brilliant venture, but
it seemed to be an equally safe one—one of those
undertakings for which the way had been paved,
but the possibilities left untested.   The idea was
to build a line of trading-posts up the Missouri
and across the Rockies to the Columbia and on
to the Pacific coast.   St. Louis was to be the
distributing-point for all posts east of the Rocky
Mountains, while the fort to be built at the mouth
of the Columbia and supplied by vessels sailing
around Cape Horn was to serve as a center for
the western posts.   The furs stored at this latter
point were to be taken by the supply vessels to
China and there exchanged for a cargo of goods
suited to the New York market.   Incidentally it
was hoped that considerable revenue would be derived from provisioning the Russian forts on the
Alaskan coasts.   To quote the rather picturesque
language of Bancroft, which is strongly tainted
by malice:

It would indeed be a smooth glittering, golden round, furs
from Astoria to Canton, teas, silks, and rich Asiatic merchandise
to New York, then back again to the Columbia with beads, and
bells, and blankets, guns, knives, tobacco, and rum.[27]

Bancroft estimates that in this ways furs could be taken to China in one-half the ordinary time, and supplies brought by vessel at one-tenth the overland cost.

In furtherance of this undertaking, the Pacific Fur Company was formed in 1810 with a capital of $200,000, divided into one hundred shares of which Astor held fifty, Hunt as his representative and chief manager, five, the other partners, four each, while the remaining shares were left to the clerks. Astor was to furnish supplies up to the amount of $400,000 and to bear all the loss for the first five years, although he agreed to share the profits.[28] As has been said, the scheme looked eminently practical. This northwest country had been explored by Lewis and Clark (1804-6)[29] and a company of St. Louis merchants had traded up the Missouri and Nebraska rivers and even built a fort west of the Rocky Mountains, from which, however, they had been

[27]Bancroft, *History of the Northwest Coast,* Vol. II, p. 139.

[28]Ross, *Adventures of the First Settlers on the Oregon or Columbia River,* p. 39.

[29]Turner, *The Fur Trade in Wisconsin,* Johns Hopkins Studies, Ninth Series, p. 71, says that the idea of the Lewis and Clark expedition was proposed to Congress by Jefferson, as a means of fostering the Indian trade. "Bearing in mind his [i. e. Jefferson's] instructions to this party that they should see whether the Oregon furs might not be shipped down the Missouri instead of passing around Cape Horn, and the relation of his early canal schemes to this design, we see he had conceived the idea of a transcontinental fur-trade which should center in Virginia."

driven by the Indians.[30]   As for the trade from
the Pacific coast to China, it has been already
shown that it had been carried on with immense
success since 1788.   So early as 1792, at least
twenty-five vessels, most of them from Boston,
were on the western coast, and Ross estimated
that they averaged a clear gain of 1,000 per cent.
every second year.   In view of the extraordinary
statements of Ross concerning his trade with the
Indians of the interior,[31] this estimate would appear by no means excessive.

The country that was to supply the Astorian
settlement with furs was, then, not altogether
unknown territory.   Very probably it would
have been worked ere this by the North West
Company (indeed they had built several forts
west of the Rocky Mountains) had it not been
that Montreal, the base of supplies, was so far
away, and they were prevented by the monopoly
of the East India Company from shipping directly to China.   That Astor feared their possible competition is evidenced by the fact that he
offered them a one-third interest in his new enterprise.   His offer being refused, he did the next
best thing—seduced some of their most experi-

---

[30]George Bryce, *The Remarkable History of the Hudson's Bay
Co.*, chap. xxii.
[31]Cf. p. 12 of this volume.

enced men into partnership with him by promising them most generous terms.[32]

As has been shown, it was not in any single feature that the Astorian scheme appeared original, although the fur-trade, at best, demanded adventurous daring—a reaching-out into new fields. But, as a great co-ordinating scheme, the plan bore witness to the organizing ability and the grasp of the man who conceived it. Its aim was distinctly monopolistic, and if it had succeeded, it would have been a disastrous blow to Astor's rivals. With New York as an outlet for the eastern posts, with Astoria as an outlet for the western ones, and with St. Louis as the feeder for the middle territory, Astor would have been infinitely better equipped than rivals who had to send supplies by land, and conduct their operations with foreign countries from a single center. Ross, a Scotchman who went on the Astorian expedition and afterward developed a bitter hostility to Astor, characterized the Pacific Fur Company as

that concern which proposed to extend its grasping influence from ocean to ocean and which, to use the projector's own words, was to have annihilated the South Company, rivaled the North West Company, extinguished the Hudson's Bay Company, driven

---

[32]Bancroft, *History of the Northwest Coast,* Vol. II, pp. 141, 142; Washington Irving, *Astoria,* pp. 35, 36.

the Russians into the Frozen Ocean, and with the resources of China to have enriched America.[33]

The plan failed, but not because of any difficulties that could have been foreseen. The War of 1812 broke out, Astor's supply ship did not arrive on time, and it was feared a British man-of-war might appear any day and demand the surrender of the fort. The partners, therefore, sold out to a representative of the North West Company for $80,500.[34] This sum seems decidedly insignificant, in view of the fact that Astor had spent over a million dollars to carry his plans into effect. There had been an overland expedition to equip, and a party to be sent by sea, with two supply vessels to follow before any news of the first one could be had. The "Tonquin," the ship which conveyed some of the partners to Astoria, was blown up after captain and crew had been massacred by the Indians of the upper coast while on a trading expedition; and a ship carrying supplies was wrecked off the Sandwich Is-

---

[33]Ross, *Adventures of the First Settlers on the Oregon or Columbia River*, p. 270.

[34]Chittenden, *The History of the American Fur Trade of the Far West*. Vol. I, chap. xii; Bancroft, *History of the Northwest Coast*, Vol. II, p. 229, notes 8 and 9.

"Mr. Astor," says Ross, "thought he was cheated because the beaver on hand was sold at $2.00, and the otter at $0.50, when these skins were bringing $5.00 or $6.00 each at Canton." However that may be, there were mutual recriminations of a more serious nature, the recital of which would not be at all pertinent to the present investigation.

lands. The cargoes were insured, however, so that
probably the worst result of these losses, financially speaking, was the disheartening effect that
they had on the men stationed at Astoria. Another ship, moreover, after provisioning Astoria,
had sailed northward to the Russian settlements
and thence directly to China, the captain refus-
ing to put in again at that post, although he had
Hunt, the chief manager, aboard. This vessel
carried furs costing $25,000 to Canton, which
would at that time have sold for $150,000, the
proceeds invested in nankeens bringing perhaps
$300,000 in New York.[35] No wonder, after such
expenditures and with such profits in anticipation, that Astor should have lamented the sale of
his interests to the North West Company at
any price they might have offered.

The check given to this plan for the development of the northwestern trade by the failure of
the Astorian scheme was effectual. It may seem
strange that Astor did not renew his attempts
upon the conclusion of the war, but it ought to
be remembered that the North West Company
retained possession of Astoria, now Fort George,
until August, 1818, and that during all this period, the northwest boundary was matter for dis-

---

[35]Bancroft, *History of the Northwest Coast,* Vol. II, p. 220.

pute. In 1818 it was agreed that a settlement of
the boundary question should be postponed for
ten years,[36] during which time the northwest
coast was to be open to subjects of both nations.
In view of the uncertainty connected with the
final disposition of this territory, as well as in
view of the fact that the North West Company
was now firmly intrenched in the region, it was
not surprising that Astor should have definitely
relinquished his plans. It should be remembered,
too, that the North West Company boasted an
organization superior to that of the American
Fur Company. Its men were highly trained, its
working arrangements thoroughly perfected, and
its dealings with the Indians subjected to definite
rules and regulations. The way in which this
company had conducted its commerce with the
natives had tended to attach them to its interests,
and whenever American traders encountered its
competition it was apt to be to their eventual
discomfiture. None knew better than Astor the
extent of the competitive resources of the North
West Company, and before attempting to carry
the Columbian plan into effect, he had tried to
secure the co-operation of these rivals. When
he failed in that, he selected men from the North

---

[36] It was not finally settled till 1846.

West Company to take charge of the undertaking, because he thought that they alone had the requisite experience and hardihood to make success possible. Their desertion, coupled with the presence in the field of the North West Company itself, meant that the American organization would have to engage, competitively speaking, in a campaign of offense under the direction of subordinates less experienced than those in the employ of the British company. Such considerations as these were, no doubt, conclusive in determining Astor not to revive his western project.

Thereafter, operations were generally confined to the middle west, but the North West Company was paid in kind for the part it played in the enforced sale of Astoria. After the conclusion of the war, John Jacob Astor employed all his political influence to procure the passage of a bill excluding foreigners from participation in the fur-trade of the United States. He was successful in this attempt and in 1816 the North West Company was forced to relinquish certain lucrative posts south of the Canadian line. Astor immediately bought up all these posts very much at his own price,[37] and in the same year organized

[37]Chittenden, *The History of the American Fur Trade of the Far West,* Vol. I, pp. 310, 311; Bancroft, *The History of the Northwest Coast,* Vol. I, p. 513; J. H. Lockwood, "Early Times and Events in Wisconsin," *Wisconsin Historical Collections,* Vol. IV, p. 102.

the American Fur Company which combined
these newly acquired possessions with those of
the South West Company incorporated just before the outbreak of the War of 1812. The incident affords an illustration of one prolific source
of wealth to the man who is already rich: the
ability to create and to take advantage of exceptional opportunities to acquire property for less
than it is worth. It is, perhaps, the same sort of
thing that occurs to-day when men of wealth slip
into the control of corporations suffering a temporary financial embarrassment. It is again a
case of forced sale; they get something for less
than it is worth, because of the pressure that has
been brought to bear upon those in possession.
And in some instances, as is well known, the purchasers have themselves been instrumental in
causing that pressure to be exerted.

At first, the American Fur Company traded
in the region of the Great Lakes, the upper Mississippi, and a tract east of Lake Huron, with
Mackinaw as its base, but gradually it extended
its territory, and in 1822 its western department
was established with headquarters at St. Louis.
This department was confined to the Missouri
River and to the lower posts on the Mississippi
and the Illinois. In 1826, it came into collision
with the Columbia Fur Company, with which it

effected a union in 1827, the name of the combination being changed to the North American Fur Company. The organization of the Columbia Company was left practically intact, it being transformed into a sub-department having charge of the trade of the Missouri above the mouth of the Big Sioux.[38]

Forsythe, in a letter to Secretary of War Cass,[39] dated 1831, gives some interesting details concerning the trade of the region dominated by the North American Company. The traders supplied the Indians in the autumn with goods on credit, before the hunting season began. As possibly not more than half the debts thus contracted were made good, the Indians were forced to pay twice the price in skins that they would have had to pay in the spring when provided with furs. The Sauk and Fox Indians (population about 6,000), wrote Forsythe, had become so entirely dependent upon the traders for their winter supplies, that they would have literally starved without them. Consequently, they were forced to make their purchases in the autumn,

---

[38]Chittenden, *The History of the American Fur Trade of the Far West;* cf. chapters dealing with the North American Fur Company in Vol. I.

[39]Cf. Chittenden, Vol. III, p. 936, for a letter from Thomas Forsythe to Lewis Cass, Secretary of War. [From the Manuscript Department of the State Historical Society of Wisconsin.]

paying exorbitant prices for the most necessary articles.[40]   If debts such as these were eventually discharged, the trader made a profit approximating 100 per cent.; but assuming that only a half or even a third of the debts were collected, the gains were still of a size to justify suspicions of exploitation.   Certainly it was a master-stroke to divert the Indians from the varied activities which made of them a self-sufficing people; induce them to become fur-trapping specialists for the benefit of the white man; and then purchase

---

[40]The following is an estimate of certain transactions, serving to show the profits of the trader under ordinary conditions:

The Indian takes credit in the autumn for

A 3-point blanket at................$10.00
A rifle gun......................... 30.00
A pound of gunpowder.............. 4.00
                                    _____
                                    $44.00

A 3-point blanket will cost in England say 16*s.*

A blanket at 100 per cent............$ 3.52
A rifle gun (at St. Louis).......12.00-13.00
A pound of gunpowder.............. 0.20
                                    _____
                                    $16.72
25 per cent. for expenses....... 4.18
                                    _____
                                    $20.90

From Forsythe's letter to Cass, Chittenden, Vol. IV, p. 926.

The trader took for a dollar a large buckskin, weighing perhaps six pounds, or two doeskins, four muskrats, four or five raccoons or allowed the Indian three dollars for an otter skin, and two dollars for one pound of beaver.

Turner, *Johns Hopkins Studies*, No. 9, states that the system of credits dates back to the French period.   Cf. also *American State Papers, Indian Affairs*, Vol. II, pp. 64-66.

their furs on credit, at prices based upon a knowledge of their superinduced economic dependence.

Turner says:

The credit system left the Indians at the mercy of the trader
when one nation monopolized the field and it compelled them to
espouse the cause of one or other when two nations contended for
supremacy over their territory. At the same time it rendered the
trade peculiarly adapted to monopoly, for when rivals competed
the trade was demoralized and the Indian frequently sold to a
new trader the furs which he had pledged in advance for the
goods of another. When the American Fur Company gained
control, they systematized matters, so that there was no competition between their own agents, and private dealers cut into their
trade but little for some years.

Indeed, the North American Fur Company was
recognized as being "the monopoly"—the organization with which every individual or group of
individuals attempting to operate independently
must expect to cope. It was not that the field
was by any means fully covered, but Astor's company operated over a sufficiently extensive region
with sufficiently large resources to enable it to
employ against its rivals every device known to
monopolistic competition. The nature of the fur-
trade was such that, as regarded actual operations in the field, the individual trader was frequently at a positive advantage in a given lo-
cality. In his direct dealings with the Indians
there was no reason why he should not make as
good a bargain as another man, and when he was

able to dispense rum (which he could more easily smuggle into the Indian country than could a prominent corporation) he was sure to get the very best of the trade.[41]

But the North American Fur Company had that never-failing resource of an extended monopoly—it could change its schedule of prices to meet the exigencies of the situation. Chittenden says:

> [It did] very much as [does] the Standard Oil Company to-day [which] crushes any rival enterprise that may dare to show its head in any part of the United States. . . . *Carte blanche* to the clerks simply meant that they might pay the Indians any price, however high, for furs, and might make use of any amount of liquor that was necessary to secure the trade.[42]

Naturally, persons operating within a limited territory could not withstand such an opposition

---

[41]The importation of liquor into the Indian country was absolutely forbidden in 1832, although the American Fur Company pleaded to use it in the territory of its foreign rivals.

[42]Chittenden, Vol. I, p. 353; Childs, *Wisconsin Historical Collections,* Vol. IV, p. 156; White, *Michigan Pioneer Collections,* Vol. XI, p. 180.

John Johnston in a letter to his sister from Fond du Lac, August 27, 1833, says that the Indians whom he told that he was conducting an expedition in opposition to the American Fur Company, "seemed pleased at the thought of opposition, but the 'Company,' they said, had used threats where milder means failed to deter them from encouraging new-comers" (Smithsonian, *Schoolcraft Papers*).

In another letter from Leech Lake, November 4, 1833, Johnston writes that although the Indians of the region kill animals whose furs amount to 100 or 130 packs, weighing from eighty to ninety pounds each, the opposition traders have never left the country with more than five or at most eight packs (Smithsonian, *Schoolcraft Papers*).

which might continue for an indefinitely long period without serious injury to the larger organization. It is just this sort of competition that causes the greatest amount of irritation to-day under a more highly developed industrial organization. It causes irritation, because it is evidence of an advantage due to size rather than efficiency. From the nature of the case the fur-trade did not permit of an excessively complex organization, as within any particular region the methods of doing business were much the same; it was a case of barter with simple people whose ignorance put them quite outside the pale of economic generalizations on the subject of exchange. The North American Fur Company was not, then, a highly integrated industrial machine whose efficiency and economy of operation offered justification for the disappearance of less fit organizations. It simply engrossed the business of other concerns because of its greater resources—a case of acquisition, pure and simple, since it introduced no innovations when once installed in the place of its rivals.

But price inequalities were not the only efficient factors in establishing the Astor monopoly. Competition could be overborne by physical expedients as well; and it was. Force and fraud were the weapons of all parties, but naturally they were weapons that could be wielded more effectively by a large corporation than by private individuals. It is not surprising that bloodshed, even murder, should figure in the competitive annals of the fur-trade. There was no effective police control save such as the trading companies themselves tried to exercise. The subordinates had been trained to habits of strife by their mode of life and for them the contest was sometimes a primitive struggle in which the economic interests involved remained very obscure. None the less, it was an effective mode of aggrandizement, redounding to the enrichment of men such as Astor who, detached from intimate connection with such affairs, would no doubt have condemned these methods in their cruder manifestations. They were, however, the natural concomitants of competition unrestrained by legal authority, and as such they come within the range of economic interest.

Another reason why competition was so disastrous was perhaps because of the fact that the risks of loss were thrown upon the company traders. The goods were furnished by Astor, at a fixed advance upon costs and charges, to the various distributing posts of the interior.[43] Here the

---

[43]"None of the traders became wealthy. Astor's company absorbed the profits. It required its clerks or factors to pay an

outfits were made up and there was a second regular advance. The chances of loss therefore all fell upon the trader and sometimes he must needs resort to desperate expedients, if he would come out with any profits. Not only did the company throw the risks upon individuals, but it has been said with a certain amount of justice, that it left to other men and other companies the task of opening up new regions, which it could afterward enter with perfect assurance that its superior resources would eventually enable it to take the field. Such a conservative policy is, of course, in interesting contrast with John Jacob Astor's

---

advance of 81½ per cent. on the sterling cost of the blankets, strouds, and other English goods in order to cover the costs of importation and the expense of transportation from New York to Mackinaw. Articles purchased in New York were charged with 15 1-3 per cent. advance for transportation and each class of purchasers was charged with 33 1-3 per cent. advance as profit on the aggregate amount." "Schoolcraft Report," *Senate Document, No. 90, Twenty-second Congress, First Session*, p. 42.

Cf. also a letter of John Johnston to his sister from Sault Ste. Marie, July 23, 1833. (Smithsonian, *Schoolcraft Papers*.) Johnston says: "The Eastern merchants furnish goods, merchandise and all necessary articles for trade at a certain percentage, with the privilege of having the first refusal of the furs obtained." The independent trader, Johnston thought, could make a fair profit, "but," he writes, "when individuals or companies were interested with the company [i. e., the company furnishing supplies] in place of 33 1-3 per cent. they charged 10 per cent. and received one-half the profits made on outfits and on receipt of the furs generally gave what they thought proper." At the outfitting posts he thinks there is scarcely any competition, the trader being compelled to take the merchandise at exorbitant charges. "To obtain and pay for goods and barely obtain a livelihood the whole weight, extortion, fraud, and deceit falls on the Indians."

early ventures. Then, he chose that field which seemed to offer the best chance of gain, and he gladly ran the risks involved for the sake of the large returns he might secure. But for a company covering a great territory whose work was done by subordinates, matters were quite otherwise. It was possible to estimate one year with another the chances of gain or loss, and to make advances to the traders on the basis of such estimates. The position of the trader was somewhat analogous to that of the Indian; he was for the time dependent upon the supplies offered him by the North American Fur Company and he must perforce accept them upon the terms granted by the company. Judging from the usual penniless condition of the trader, the American Fur Company must have gained considerably more than it would have gained had it not shifted the risks.

By 1834, Astor's fur interests had become of slight moment in comparison with his immense real estate holdings, and he was, moreover, getting too old for active participation in the work of direction. Consequently, in the year named he sold out his interests in the Northern Department of the American Fur Company to Ramsay Crooks and his associates, while the western department was taken over by Pratte, Chouteau & Company, of St. Louis. Chittenden suggests that this move may have been dictated by certain purely economic considerations which do credit to his business astuteness. In proof, he cites a statement in a letter from Astor written from London the summer before the sale of his interests: "I much fear," he writes, "beaver will not sell well very soon unless very fine. It appears that they make hats of silk instead of beaver." But it was probably not from the point of view of demand alone that the fur-trade showed signs of decline. The supply of furs was also becoming scarcer and the expenses connected with the trade were increasing as it became necessary to push the trading-posts farther west. William B. Astor, writing to the Secretary of War in response to inquiries concerning the state of trade, says:

On the frontiers the deer and other large animals have nearly disappeared, and in that region a great reduction is also visible in the number of those which are valuable for their fur. But in what may more properly be called "the Indian country" there is but little diminution of late years, and what the advance of the whites annually takes away is almost made good by the extension of our trading-posts, more particularly toward the Rocky Mountains; so that if we have less of one thing, we have more of another, and the annual value of our aggregate returns is pretty much the same.[44]

It will be noticed that William Astor's statement contains several reservations. He alleges

[44]Senate Document, No. 90, Twenty-second Congress, First Session, p. 77.

4

that the trade is "almost" made good, and the
value of the aggregate returns he affirms to be
"pretty much the same."

Schoolcraft writing in 1836 says of northern
Michigan:

> The value of the fur-trade in this portion of the country is
> one of questionable character, at the present era. Large sums
> have formerly been made as well as lost in its prosecution. But
> more than nine-tenths of the whole avails of this trade have been
> sent to seaboard or foreign markets and have not enriched the
> resident inhabitants. This trade is yearly diminishing and it may
> perhaps be added, the sooner it is extinct and both the white men
> and Indians employ themselves in regular industry the better.[45]

It is evident from the foregoing statements
that the country furnishing the American Fur
Company with the main portion of its supplies
was becoming rapidly populated and therefore
unfit territory for the hunter. Moreover, the region toward the mountains could only be exploited at an increased expense, and in the face

---

[45]In the Appendix of Washington Irving's *Astoria* (Philadelphia ed., 1873), p. 640, appears an article entitled, "Notices of the
Present State of the Fur-Trade Chiefly Extracted from an Article
Published in *Silliman's Magazine* for June, 1834." It is there
stated that "it appears that the fur-trade must henceforward
decline. The advanced state of geographical science shows that
no new countries remain to be explored. In North America the
animals are slowly decreasing from the persevering efforts and the
indiscriminate slaughter practised by the hunters and by the
appropriation to the uses of man of those forests and rivers
which have afforded them food and protection. They recede with
the aborigines before the tide of civilization, but a diminished
supply will remain in the mountains and uncultivated tracts of
this and other countries, if the avidity of the hunter can be
restrained within **proper limitations.**"

of a competition which was practically non-existent for the Astor interests in the middle west. If John Jacob Astor were cognizant of all these facts, they were no doubt a more potent influence than old age in effecting his withdrawal from the trade. The chances are that he, in common with many men of large fortune, was just as eager to scent signs of decay as he was quick to detect evidences of potential prosperity; just as opportune in withdrawing from a declining venture, as timely in undertaking any new enterprise that promised growth.

II.

Thus far only the trading ventures of John Jacob Astor have been discussed. But it is not therefore to be inferred that they were the sole species of gain-getting with which Astor was identified. In fact, it is well known that the returns derived from trade were quantitatively a comparatively insignificant portion of the great fortune which he transmitted to his descendants, the bulk of that fortune being derived from real-estate investments in and around New York City. Nevertheless, the profits that grew out of Astor's early operations in the fur-trade and in foreign shipping afforded the means necessary for embarkation upon his policy of land investment. Consequently, the initial stages in the development of his trading interests gain added significance as the indispensable antecedents of a later era of bewilderingly rapid expansion of wealth.

As early as 1800 Astor adopted the policy of utilizing his mercantile gains in the purchase of land just beyond the city limits. He gradually sold this land as its price advanced, in order that more extensive tracts somewhat farther out might be bought with the proceeds. Parton tells a story that serves to illustrate his methods. In 1810, it is said, Astor sold a lot near Wall Street for $8,000—a sale highly pleasing to the purchaser, who averred that in a few years it would be worth $12,000. "Yes," said Astor, "but with the $8,000 I will buy eighty lots above Canal Street, and by that time my lots will be worth $80,000."

It was somewhat prior to the date of this prudent sale that Astor bought up the rights of succession to certain lands in Putnam County[46]—a purchase destined to bring his name into rather

---

[46]Cf. Parton, *Life of John Jacob Astor*. Cf. also, *Niles' Register,* February 27, 1819; June 7, 1828; March 20, 1830; June 26, 1830. Cf. also, the case of Jackson vs. Carver, Circuit Court of the United States for the Southern District of New York. Reported by E. V. Sparhawk for the *New York American*. Publisher, Elam Bliss, New York, 1827.

unpleasant repute. At the outbreak of the Revolutionary War about one-third of the lands in Putnam County had been held by Roger and Mary Morris, but, as they were loyalists, their holdings had been declared attainted, and had been taken over by the state. In some way, John Jacob Astor learned that the Morrises had possessed only a life-interest in the property, and that upon their death their heirs could still inherit it, the attainder not operating to divest the latter of their rights of succession. Astor thereupon purchased the rights of the heirs (1809) for the sum of $100,000. At the time about seven hundred families were settled on the property, residing there under titles given them by the state, and quite ignorant of the fact that they were in imminent danger of dispossession. Some years later, there was great consternation when Astor made known his claims, and the state legislature at once appointed commissioners to inquire into the matter and see what could be done. At that period the lands in dispute were conceded to be worth $667,-000, but Astor's offer to settle with the state for $300,000 was nevertheless refused. Thereupon, negotiations were dropped, not to be renewed until 1818. Roger Morris had then been some time dead, and his widow was advanced in years and very feeble. Consequently, it was evident

that the ownership of their former estate would
soon vest in the purchaser of the rights of succession.   The matter of a settlement was again
agitated, and this time Astor offered to take
$300,000 with interest for the four years that
had elapsed since his first offer.   But once more
he met with a refusal, and no further action was
taken until 1827, when the legislature enacted a
law which provided that Astor should be offered
a certain price for his claims, if, within thirty
days, he executed a deed of conveyance in fee simple to the state, with a warranty against the
claims of the Morris heirs.[47]   However, before he
could receive any part of the sum agreed upon,
he must obtain a judgment of the United States
Supreme Court in favor of his title.

In 1830, Astor's claims were sustained by a decision of the Supreme Court in the first one of
five suits, which, it had been arranged, should be
prosecuted to a final judgment.   It had also been
agreed that, if three of these suits should be decided in his favor, he was to receive from the
state $450,000 in payment of his rights, subject
to a deduction of $200,000, in case the court held
that buildings and improvements did not go
with the ownership of the land in dispute.   In

---

[47]Mary Morris had died before this last-named date.

June, 1830, a third verdict was rendered which meant victory for Astor. He received the full amount of $450,000, with interest from April, 1827, for a property which by that time had attained a valuation of $1,500,000. The sturdiness with which this claim was pushed to a successful issue in the face of vituperation shows the character of the man. Judging from such evidence, it would certainly seem that he was devoid of those non-commercial and extra-legal standards of right-dealing which hinder many men in their advance toward fortune.[48] The incident obviously brings out traits of disposition which have undoubtedly been important factors in the acquisition of wealth by individuals such as he.

During the War of 1812 Astor loaned large sums on real estate security and had numerous opportunities to foreclose the mortgages thus ac-

---

[48]In one of the early suits that came to trial in the United States District Court for the Southern District of New York (Jackson vs. Carver, 1827,), the case for the tenants holding under the State was argued by Webster, who made a straight appeal to the prejudices of his hearers, since he had a very weak legal defense. "The lands to be affected by a verdict in this case were held as a patrimony by the defendants. They had purchased them from the original patentee; they had labored for years to improve them. The rugged hills had grown green under their cultivation before a question was raised as to the integrity of their titles. They have grown with the lands around them and they have a right to retain them until a legal claimant comes to turn them out of possession. And unless the testimony upon which that individual founds his claim is as clear as possible it is your duty to reject his title and retain the lands in the hands in which they now are."

quired under conditions most favorable to himself.   Likewise, during the panic of 1837, when real estate was a drug on the market, he reaped an unprecedented harvest.   At that time he is said to have appeared as a complainant in some sixty different suits, in nearly every case obtaining valuable properties at absurdly low prices.

But it was not only during periods of financial distress that Astor secured extraordinary bargains.   His ability to diagnose probable future developments enabled him at all times to buy for insignificant sums unimproved or remote properties, which later came to be valued at many times the prices originally paid for them.[49]   For instance, William Waldorf Astor says, when speaking of his great-grandfather's investments in real estate:

---

[49]For instance, $2,000 is said to have been the purchase price of a block in Harlem worth $1,000,000 to-day.   Numerous lots on lower Broadway, bought at various times for $200 or $300, are now estimated to be worth from $300,000 to $400,000.   An East Side farm that cost Astor $20,000 has a present-day valuation of $8,000,000.   For $75,000 he purchased one-half of Governor Clinton's Greenwich estate.   Later Clinton's son-in-law borrowed money of Astor on the security of real estate, which was eventually taken over by the latter for non-payment of debt.   Nearly two-thirds of the Clinton property thus came into possession of the Astor family, which to-day, it is estimated, derives a yearly income of $500,000 from the buildings erected upon it.

These details are taken quite uncritically from an article by Burton Hendrick in *McClure's Magazine*, April, 1905.   There seems no reason for doubting their substantial truth, however, and they gain added credence in the light of the statement made by William Waldorf Astor in an article in the *Pall Mall Magazine*, Vol. XVIII.

These purchases were made with such judgment in the line
of approaching expansion as frequently to be sold again after a
few years for double or treble what he paid for them. One of
these farms purchased in 1811 for $900 is now worth, with its
improvements, $1,400,000.[50]

A discussion of the immense gains derived by
John Jacob Astor from land investments must
not lose sight of the fact that those investments
were made under peculiarly propitious circumstances. They were begun when the land was
young and relatively undeveloped, and they per-
sisted during a period of extraordinary growth—
a period during which New York was assuming
ever greater importance as the commercial center
of a country whose trade and industry were advancing by leaps and bounds. The rapid appre-
ciation of land-values which took place could
hardly have occurred in an older community,
where conditions are more stable and development progresses at a steadier pace. Moreover,
in an old country there is not the same tendency
to sudden shifts of the commercial centre of grav-
ity, as there is in a new one, whose resources are
being continually developed, and whose facilities
for transport are being improved. For instance,
the completion of the Erie Canal in 1825 at once
threw a large part of the western trade, which had

---

[50]*Pall Mall Magazine,* Vol. XVIII.

formerly gone through Baltimore and Philadelphia, toward New York; and, in addition, it led to an increase in the amount of products carried, since it so cheapened the cost of transportation as to bring new lands toward the northwest into the market.[51] There would, of course, be every reason to expect a rapid augmentation of the population, trade, and land values of New York City, as a result of these changes. The statistics of growth of the period from 1820 to 1850 are indeed astonishing,[52] and it is not surprising, in the light of

---

[51]Andrews, *Report on the Colonial and Lake Trade*, 1852, pp. 275, 276.

[52]Statistics showing the amount of the imports and exports of New York City for a series of years bear excellent witness to its unusual growth as a center of foreign shipping, and these statistics are especially significant when compared with the figures for Boston and Philadelphia, both of which cities at one time excelled New York in the magnitude of their foreign shipments. The value of the imports into Boston, Philadelphia, and New York for the period from 1820 to 1850, are as follows:

	Boston.	Philadelphia.	New York.
1820		$8,150,000	$26,020,000
1830		9,520,000	38,650,000
1840	$14,820,000	8,460,000	60,060,000
1850	28,650,000	12,060,000	116,660,000

The value of the exports are:

	Boston.	Philadelphia.	New York.
1820		$5,740,000	$11,760,000
1830		4,290,000	17,660,000
1840	$8,230,000	6,820,000	32,400,000
1850	9,140,000	4,500,000	47,580,000

The population of the city grew during this period from 123,700 in 1820 to 515,300 in 1850.

the development that took place, that John Jacob Astor who began to invest in real estate in 1800, when New York was little more than a good-sized town, should have died seized of holdings valued at from $18,000,000 to $20,000,000.[53]

In conclusion, it should be said that information regarding the nature and extent of John Jacob Astor's real-estate holdings is very scanty, and frequently of doubtful authenticity. The tax records of New York City throw no light on

---

Statistics showing the increase in value of the real and personal estate held within New York City are as follows:

1824	$83,070,000
1830	125,280,000
1840	252,230,000
1850	286,080,000

These figures are, however, practically worthless for purposes of comparison, as the methods of valuation varied widely from year to year. Moreover, the increase in the extent of the city lands is not known, and consequently there are no means of estimating the amount of the "unearned increment" accruing to a fixed area during this period. Then, too, personal property as well as realty is included in the estimates. Cf. Andrews, *Report on the Colonial and Lake Trade* (1852), pp. 282-88.

[53] Having acquired an immense landed estate, it was no part of Astor's purpose to make all the improvements upon it himself. He frequently rented out lands for twenty-one-year periods upon a net basis of 5 or 6 per cent., leaving to the tenants the erection of dwellings, payment of taxes, and making of repairs, the buildings and other improvements to become the property of the owner of the land upon the expiration of the lease. In consequence of the hard terms exacted, large blocks of land, it is said, were left vacant or else covered with the flimsiest sort of structures. Cf. Burton Hendrick, "The Astor Fortune," *McClure's Magazine*, April, 1905.

the subject,[54] and no definite knowledge is to be got from a study of Astor's will, since, after making various minor bequests, chiefly of land, he devises the rest of his property without further specification to his son, William B. Astor.[55] Detailed information is therefore lamentably lacking, but the facts that are obtainable will, it is thought, prove sufficient to furnish material for certain broad generalizations, and to afford the data necessary for purposes of comparison with other phases of Astor's activity.

---

[54]The tax records of the city of New York give no information concerning the ownership of the parcels of real estate assessed. The president of the Board of Tax Commissioners of New York City (Borough of Manhattan) thinks that the only way to obtain even a partial knowledge of the extent of the real-estate holdings of John Jacob Astor is to undertake an elaborate search through the records in the County Register's office.

[55]Parton, *Life of John Jacob Astor,* to which is appended a copy of his will. The only investments mentioned in the will other than those in real estate are as follows: $100,000 in New York City 5 per cent. bonds; $50,000 in New Haven 5½ per cent. bonds; certain sums deposited in the New York Life Insurance and Trust Co.; 500 shares of the capital stock of the Bank of North America; 1,000 shares of the Manhattan Co.; 1,000 shares of the capital stock of the Merchants' Bank; 1,604 shares of the capital stock of the Mechanics Bank. These scattered items are probably of no great significance for present purposes.

CHAPTER III.

THE FORTUNE OF JAY GOULD.

I.

JAY GOULD prefaced his speculative activities by a short probation as clerk in a hardware store, a lengthier experience as surveyor of county lands, and a three years' career as tanner in western Pennsylvania.[1] In this last occupation he laid the first slight foundations of his subsequent prosperity, and from it he derived, in part at least, the funds employed in his early speculative ventures. It is not altogether clear just how Gould succeeded in establishing himself in the tanning industry, although it is easy enough to see how he might have acquired some knowledge of the business as he explored the tanning regions of New York and Pennsylvania on his surveying expeditions. At any rate, he somehow managed to secure the co-operation of a wealthy tanner, Colonel Pratt, of Prattsville, with whose assistance he was enabled to install himself as head of

---

[1]For details of his early life, cf. an article on Jay Gould in *Sketches of Men of Progress,* (1870-71). Cf. also Houghton, *Kings of Fortune,* (1888). Both of these accounts contain manifest inaccuracies and conflicting statements. Cf. also articles in the New York *Times* for December 3, 1892.

a large concern in western Pennsylvania. One
writer implies that the alluring prospects of gain
afforded by that untouched western region were
so ably presented by Gould, that Pratt was at
once induced to join in this venture.[2] Another
biographer insinuates that a timely dose of flat-
tery did the work. He states that Gould, while
editor of a newspaper for a short time in 1856,
wrote an article urging Pratt's nomination to the
Vice-Presidency—to the great delight of that
unsophisticated gentleman. In fact, Pratt was
so pleased that he cheerfully agreed to take Gould
with him to western Pennsylvania, where he proceeded to purchase acres of forest land, and to
erect a tannery, surrendering to Gould, as his
partner, full charge of the whole.[3]

However chimerical the accounts of its origin,
the tannery was actually built, and, under
Gould's management, was soon prospering. The
company weathered the panic of 1857, and two
years later Gould bought out Pratt's interest
in the business. The events leading up to this
purchase are again obscure. It has been said (although such unsubstantiated statements must be
taken with caution) that Pratt became convinced
that Gould was using the firm's signature for

---

[2]Cf. article in *Sketches of Men of Progress*.
[3]Cf. the article in Houghton's *Kings of Fortune*.

borrowing sums of money, which were not used in the business.[4] Pratt, therefore, gave Gould the option of buying the entire tannery, or else of selling his interest in it. Thinking Gould unable to effect a purchase, Pratt offered to dispose of his own share of the business at a very low price. Gould was not slow to seize the opportunity of acquiring such a bargain. He obtained the necessary funds from Charles M. Leupp and Company, leather dealers of New York, and Leupp at once superseded Pratt as his partner in the tannery. But trouble of some sort speedily arose between the new partners. There was a veritable fight for possession of the tannery. The sheriff and his posse once captured the place during Gould's absence, but the latter, nothing daunted, called together his employees and ousted the invaders.[5] Thus early in Gould's career, it became necessary to employ military phraseology in describing his business tactics. Throughout his life, indeed, he displayed a fine fighting spirit, strengthened by the conviction that "all is permitted" which can be successfully accomplished. But whatever the rights of this early contest, Leupp was, at any rate, vanquished, and he speedily died or else committed suicide as a result

---

[4] *Ibid.*

[5] The New York *Times,* December 3, 1892.

of his business losses. Financial embarrassments
necessitated keeping the tannery closed for a
time, but it was soon reopened with Gould, as
sole manager and proprietor, employing two
hundred and fifty men and manufacturing
1,500,000 pounds of sole leather annually.

However, the tannery proved to be but a lever-
age for Gould's later speculative operations. At
the beginning of the sixties, railroad securities
were greatly depressed in value, and bankrupt
roads were numerous. Gould hit upon the
scheme that was to make his fortune. He aban-
doned the tannery, and, with the proceeds from
the business, together with borrowed funds, he
began to invest in the shares of bankrupt companies. Among his earliest purchases were the
mortgage bonds of the Rutland and Washington,
and the Troy and Rutland railroads.[6] Not only
did Gould succeed in raising above par the bonds
which he bought at 10, but, according to his own
testimony, he actually sold some of the stock at
125.[7] In less than two years, these roads were
consolidated with the Saratoga, Whitehall and
Rensselaer, whose bonds and stocks were market-

[6]Cf. article in the New York *Times,* December 3, 1892, *Gould's
Eventful Life;* also account in *Sketches of Men of Progress.*

[7]U. S. Pacific Railway Commission, Senate Executive Docu-
ments, 51 First Session, Fiftieth Congress, Testimony of Jay
Gould, Vol. I, p. 479.

ed at a profit, the proceeds being used to purchase a large interest in the Cleveland and Pittsburgh.[8] Its securities were likewise disposed of later at an advance.

By this time, Gould was definitively established as a broker, doing business in Wall Street. In 1860, he had become acquainted with Henry W. Smith, and, shortly afterwards, they, together with Henry H. Martin, had formed the brokerage firm of Smith, Gould, and Martin.[9] Throughout the war, the partners transacted a lucrative business in railway securities, and also made money on gold speculations. The operations in gold, begun thus early, culminated several years later in the spectacular panic of September 24, 1869—"Black Friday"—the outcome of Gould's attempt to corner the gold market. The premium on gold, which had arisen as the result of the inconvertible "greenback" issues occasioned by the war, had dropped to 30 1-4 by March, 1869. This was the lowest point which had been reached in three years, and there were indications that the quotations might go still lower. But about the middle of April Gould bought seven millions of gold and put up the quotation from 132 to 140. On May 20, the quota-

---

[8] New York *Times,* December 3, 1892, *Gould's Eventful Life.*
[9] New York *Times,* December 3, 1892.

5

tion was $144\frac{7}{8}$, but in July it had fallen to
136.[10] Neither then, nor later in his career, was
Gould desirous of trusting to the luck of the
market. His plans had been laid with an elaborate caution, and he was resolved to guard
against all untoward events. If, for instance, the
government were to sell gold at a critical juncture in his "bull" campaign, the market would be
spoiled and his schemes frustrated. Gould and
his able ally, Fisk, took occasion, therefore, to
question the President of the United States concerning his views on the propriety of advancing
the premium on gold. The time selected for in-
terrogation was propitious, as Fisk had secured
the President as a guest on board his yacht, and
had exerted his lively imagination to the utmost
to afford him proper entertainment. However,
his adroit inquiries elicited little information; the
President's attitude was noncommital, not to say
discouraging.[11]

But Gould was not to be balked. He induced
Corbin, the President's brother-in-law, to mediate

[10]Report of the Committee on Banking and Currency appointed "to investigate the causes that led to the unusual and
extraordinary fluctuations of gold in the city of New York, from
the 21st to the 27th of September, 1869." House of Representatives, Report No. 31, 41st Congress, 2nd Session, p. 2.

[11]House Report, No. 31, p. 3. Cf. also Henry Adams, *The
New York Gold Conspiracy*, from *Chapters of Erie and Other
Essays*, p. 116,

in his interest, and he secured the coöperation of General Butterfield, Assistant Treasurer at New York.[12] According to Gould's own testimony, corroborated by the stammering and conflicting statements of these paid agents, he bought and carried for Corbin about two millions, and for Butterfield, about a million and a half of gold. Butterfield was also invited to join him in purchasing control of the Tenth National Bank, over half of whose capital stock was bought August 5, 1869, as preliminary to operations on the Gold Exchange.[13] Still with the desire of ensuring the success of his plans, Gould caused an article to be published in the New York *Times*, purporting to be written by a person in the intimate confidence of the President, and intending to convey the idea that the Administration would oppose a sale of gold in the interests of lower prices.[14]

[12] *The New York Gold Conspiracy*, p. 116.

[13] House Report 31; cf. testimony of Gould, pp. 151-54, and 160-64; testimony of Butterfield, pp. 314-28; testimony of Corbin, pp. 253-57.

[14] House Report 31, p. 278.
The New York *Times* refused to print a portion of the article. The excluded part read as follows:
"It may be objected that the disbursement of currency to the largest convenient extent, and the retention in the Treasury of unneeded gold, will cause gold to rise again to 135 or 140. Suppose it should thus result. It would secure large shipments of breadstuffs, provisions, butter, cheese, petroleum, cotton, tobacco, etc., at increased prices; and, to the amount shipped, would save to our people an equal value of gold. Hence, as gold accumulated, the less would be the premium upon it; high prices

Everything was done to inculcate a belief that
gold ought to rise—that the premium on it ought
to be advanced for the sake of the oppressed
farmer whose crops could then be brought to
market and disposed of at higher currency prices.
Nevertheless, it was the general belief among im-
porting merchants that gold was sure to fall.
They reasoned that an unusually large cotton
crop, payment of interest on the national debt,
and other causes would operate to keep exchange
in favor of the United States and to reduce the
premium on gold.[15] Consequently, nearly all of
the large importers were "short" of the market.
If they could be "cornered," Gould would be
able to profit at the expense of many wealthy
victims.

---

for gold *before the sale of our products* would cause lower prices
of gold after the sale of exports. It is better for our country to
ship produce to pay for our imports than gold or bonds. The
objection to the retention of gold in the Treasury until our
productions are marketed is unsound; for the retention of gold
will make both gold and the productions dearer at the time of the
sale of the productions; if gold is not needed for shipment, the
premium on it would fall. Large exports of produce, stimulated
by the temporary high price of gold, would cause gold to bear a
lower price. Hence, a high price for gold, during the next three
months, would be productive of great good to exporters of produce. The fall of gold at this time to 25 per cent. would bring
ruin upon the agricultural, manufacturing, and mechanical
classes; injury to these would entail injury upon the merchants
and upon laborers. If gold is made cheap, it will be exported;
if too dear to export, then produce will be shipped in lieu of it.
Hence government will not so act as to lessen the value of this
year's abundant crop, but will labor to increase its value and pro-
mote its exportation to foreign countries."

[15]House Report 31, p. 332. Testimony of Mr. Opdyke.

Fisk did not definitively join the gold clique till the middle of September, when he became convinced that the Administration was engaged in speculation, and that success was therefore a "sure thing." It is an interesting fact that not even to a man so intimately associated with him as was Fisk, did Gould divulge the real state of affairs. The reasons for his habitual secrecy frequently became painfully apparent in the sequel. Then it was seen how little he scrupled to profit at the expense of his allies, when his opponents were getting the better of him.

By the twenty-second of September the clique had advanced the price of gold to 140½. Fisk says they had then contracted for fifty or sixty millions; Gould modestly places the amount at twenty-five millions; but Smith, his partner, estimates that their holdings ranged from forty to fifty-five millions, the purchases being made by fifty or sixty brokers. Until the twenty-third of September, the business was done through the firm of Smith, Gould, and Martin, who employed all these other brokers.[16] So soon as the clique bought gold, they loaned it to the "bears," thus receiving back the money they had given for it, compelling their opponents to pay them interest

---

[16]*Commercial and Financial Chronicle,* Oct. 16, 1869, Vol. IX, p. 486.

for the privilege of carrying it, and, as the price advanced, calling up margins, with which to purchase additional sums.[17]

Meantime Gould had waxed apprehensive. He feared Boutwell, the Secretary of the Treasury, might be induced to sell gold; so he persuaded Corbin to write the President a letter urging noninterference by the government. This communication reached President Grant at a remote spot, whither he had gone for a vacation, the messenger who brought it showing evidence of having traveled in haste. Consequently, suspicions were aroused, and Corbin was warned of the danger of engaging in gold speculations. Thoroughly alarmed at the result of his communication, Corbin reported everything to Gould and demanded a settlement. The latter was at once convinced that the game was up, and he resolved to sell out as unostentatiously and as expeditiously as possible, leaving Fisk and his *confrères* in entire ignorance of recent developments.[18]

---

[17]*Ibid.*, p. 486.

[18]Cf. Henry Adams, *The New York Gold Conspiracy*, in *Chapters of Erie and Other Essays*, pp. 124-127; also House Report 31, p. 13.

C. E. Quincey, clerk for William Heath and Co., testified to having bought over $14,015,000 of gold. Between September 11th and September 19th, he sold for the personal account of Gould, $3,845,000; sold, delivered, and settled for Smith, Gould, and Martin, the balance of the $14,015,000.

On Thursday gold closed at 144, the clique having calls for over one hundred millions. There were not more than fifteen millions of gold and certificates in New York, outside the Sub-Treasury, and at least two hundred and fifty firms, many of them leading banking and mercantile houses, were short of the market. In the midst of the prevailing excitement, Gould continued to buy small amounts, merely to keep up appearances, while selling all the time through agents to the very brokers who thought they were purchasing in his interest. William Belden, the tool of his machinations, gave unlimited orders, referring to Fisk and to Smith, Gould, and Martin, as his principals.[19] Moreover, Albert Speyers, convinced that Belden was broker for the whole party, was induced to buy on behalf of the latter. Before noon of the eventful Friday, Speyers had purchased nearly sixty millions of gold, and Belden did not even know how much had been bought in his name. At the height of the hysterical confusion precipitated by all this reckless buying, James Brown, a banker, who was leading in the "bear" interest those men whose legitimate business required the purchase of gold, offered a million at 162. Doubt seized his opponents;

[19]House Report 31, pp. 12, 13.

there were no takers. Then the same amount was offered at 161; finally, five millions at 160. Thereupon the market broke, and ten minutes later came the news that the government had ordered General Butterfield to sell four millions of gold, and to purchase four millions of bonds.[20] Upon the receipt of that information, the price plunged downward to 133. The "corner" had so little basis in reality, that it had succumbed without perceptible delay to the shock occasioned by this slight blow.

It is not possible to say just how much was won or lost as a result of this attempt to "corner" gold. James B. Hodgskin, testifying before the House Committee which investigated the causes of the panic, estimated that the clique profit was $12,000,000.[21] This estimate was based on private statements made by brokers the day of the panic. Had the Friday transactions been settled, Hodgskin thought that at least twenty millions would have been lost. Gould had, indeed, nominally fulfilled all his contracts, since he had been consistently selling and making settlements at the prevailing high prices. However,

---

[20]Gould was undoubtedly anticipating such action on the part of the government. National bank examiners had previously descended upon the Tenth National Bank, and destroyed its usefulness by preventing further certifications of brokers' checks.

[21]House Report 31; testimony of James B. Hodgskin, p. 39.

he had permitted Fisk to go on buying, and had deliberately fostered the idea that they were acting in concert. Thereby Fisk and his brokers became the victims through whose agency Gould was enabled to unload his holdings.[22] However, the victimized ones did not suffer greatly. Fisk cheerfully repudiated the seventy millions of purchases made by Belden, denying that the latter had bought in his interest. In fact, Fisk even produced a letter purporting to be from Belden, telling him to purchase and sell gold on his (Belden's) account.[23] Thus the latter was made the scapegoat of the whole affair, but, as his acquiescence in this role was no doubt liberally rewarded, he is scarcely deserving of sympathy. On September 27th, Gould and Fisk, as sole answer to insistent demands for settlement, obtained twelve injunctions and judicial orders of various sorts. Thereby they placed the gold clearing house in the hands of receivers, restrained its officers from making settlements except on order of the courts, and prevented the officers of the Gold Exchange from enforcing against the clique rules to compel settlement.

---

[22]Whether Fisk remained in ignorance of Gould's plans until the very end, or whether they entered into some agreement prior to the day of the panic, is uncertain; cf., however, the Commercial and Financial Chronicle, Oct. 1869, p. 486.

[23]Cf. House Report 31; testimony of Belden, p. 301.

Fisk's testimony before the House Committee, which investigated the occurrences leading up to "Black Friday," is extremely amusing.

> The whole movement was based upon a desire on our part to employ our men, and work our power, getting the surplus crops moved east, and receiving for ourselves that portion of the transportation properly belonging to our road (i. e., the Erie). That was the beginning of the movement, and the further operations were based upon a promise of what Corbin said the government would do....My transactions were merely to support the gold market, without any understanding that there was to be any corner; without any understanding whatever, of any name oi nature, further than to assist Mr. Gould in this transaction. He had started out with the view of giving work for our men and our power during the fall and winter.[24]

Thus was a desire to profit the Erie, through the increased freightage that supposedly would come with high prices of agricultural products, alleged to be responsible for the whole movement. And, no doubt, the Erie was a very efficient cause of these operations, in that its obliging Treasury was always at the disposal of Gould and Fisk. For that matter, they would have been quite capable of maintaining that to use its funds in such a cause was to expend them legitimately in the interests of the road. But however altruistic their professed motives, their machinations resulted in a severe financial crisis. Not only speculators suffered from their attempts to "corner" gold, but the

---

[24]House Report 31, p. 176.

mercantile classes also lost heavily, as a result of the extraordinary monetary derangement that ensued.

The history of Gould's connection with the Erie dates back several years prior to his speculations in gold. His attention was first called to this road by Daniel Drew,[25] the great "bear" operator, who was one of the customers of Smith, Gould, and Martin. Drew induced Gould to join in the fight against Vanderbilt, who was making desperate efforts to secure the Erie. Indeed, Vanderbilt was determined to get possession of this, the only great line of railroad save his own, which crossed the state of New York. Early in 1868, therefore, he started out to buy control, and, astute man though he was, he was deluded into believing that he had succeeded. But he had reckoned without the resourceful Drew and his clever associates. At a most critical juncture, the Executive Committee of the Erie, of which Drew, Fisk, and Gould were all members, authorized an issue of ten millions of convertible bonds. These bonds were placed on the market in two installments. They were immediately bought in by the men in control of the Erie management, and were forthwith converted into

---

[25]New York *Times,* December 3, 1892.

stock, which was offered for sale to Vanderbilt's unsuspecting agents. Down went the stock quotations, as soon as it became known that the market had been flooded with these new issues. Vanderbilt was forced to keep buying in a vain effort to protect holdings previously bought at high prices. His losses were heavy; Drew and his fellow directors were triumphant.[26] Nevertheless, the victorious party had to flee to New Jersey to avoid processes of contempt for having disobeyed an injunction not to convert the second installment of bonds into stock.

However, Drew soon tired of loitering in New Jersey, and after the Albany legislature had passed a bill forbidding any connection between the Erie and the New York Central (May, 1868),[27] both Vanderbilt and he were prepared to come to terms. The settlement, as agreed upon, provided that Vanderbilt was to be relieved of 50,000 shares of the Erie at 70, receiving in payment $2,500,000 in cash, and $1,250,000 in bonds of the Boston, Hartford and Erie at 80. Further, he was to receive $1,000,000 as a consideration for the privilege of calling for his remain-

---

[26]Cf. Charles Francis Adams, *A Chapter of Erie,* in *Chapters of Erie and Other Essays,* pp. 29, 30.

[27]*Commercial and Financial Chronicle,* May 9, 1868, Vol. VI, p. 587. Cf. *A Chapter of Erie,* pp. 48-56, for a description of the part played by Gould in securing the passage of this bill.

ing 50,000 shares of stock at 70, any time within the following four months. He was also to have two seats on the Erie directorate placed at his disposal. Drew, for his part, was to pay into the Treasury of the Erie $540,000 with interest, as an indemnity for his peculations while Treasurer of the road. Otherwise, he was left in undisturbed possession of the gains made out of his recent extraordinary operations in the stock market.[28]

Drew now abdicated his position as Treasurer of the Erie, and Gould and Fisk were left in a position of unbridled control. During the period from July 1st, 1868, to October 24th of that year the stock of the road was increased from $34,-265,300 to $57,766,300—235,000 shares in all. Stock quotations fell rapidly and soon sales were being made at 35. This steady stream of new issues (made possible under the elastic provisions concerning convertible bonds), so completely demoralized the stock market, and placed so large an amount of the loanable funds of the community in the hands of a few speculators, that the government was forced to promise to relieve the stringency, if necessary.[29]

---

[28]*A Chapter of Erie,* p. 59. Cf. *The Commercial and Financial Chronicle* for notices appearing at intervals during the progress of the contest.

[29]*Commercial and Financial Chronicle,* Nov. 14, 1868, Vol. VII, *The Wall Street Crisis.*

Meanwhile, Daniel Drew was engaged in his usual "bearing" operations, having contracted to deliver 70,000 shares of Erie at 38 in the following November. The chance of "cornering" Drew was too good to be missed, and Gould, together with his erratic running mate, resolved to make the most of it. From having worked for a fall, they reversed their plans with a bewildering suddenness, and began to "boom" the depressed stock of their road. The task was not difficult, since the treasury of the Erie was at their disposal, and its funds could be used in making unlimited purchases. Drew, in desperation at seeing the stock slowly rising, resolved to bring suit against the management. On his affidavit, a complaint was filed by Belmont and others against the Erie Railway Company. It was urged that the parties in control of the road had secured their position by offering President Eldridge special inducements to resign, purchasing from him, at 80, $5,000,000 of bonds of the Boston, Hartford, and Erie, in which he was largely interested. Moreover, it was charged that Gould had used several millions of the funds of the company in purchasing stock and proxies prior to the October election. Finally, it was stated that, since the election, additional stock issues to the amount of $23,000,000 had been put forth, and

the money arising from the sales had been used
by the managers to further their stock speculation.[30]

In anticipation of this suit, Gould and Fisk
forestalled the application for a receivership,
which accompanied it, and induced Judge Bar-
nard, who was always at their service, to appoint
Gould receiver for the road. The latter was even
empowered to use his discretion in buying up, at
any price below par, 200,000 shares of stock,
the legality of whose issue had been quite properly
questioned. These shares, issued under the "convertible bond" provisions, had been marketed at
40, and were then selling at 35.[31] The price of
the Erie stock rose rapidly, when it became
known that the money in the treasury was being
squandered upon its purchase. Drew fought des-
perately, although his destruction appeared inevitable. However, at the very moment when it
seemed certain that Gould and Fisk had cornered
the market, large amounts of stock, supposed to
be out of the country, were offered for sale. If
the corner were to succeed, Gould and Fisk must
take all that was offered. For some reason, they

[30]*Commercial and Financial Chronicle,* November 14, 1868, Vol.
VII, p. 648.

[31]Charles Francis Adams, *A Chapter of Erie,* in *Chapters
of Erie and Other Essays,* p. 73.

failed. Drew made good his contracts at 57, and the stock fell speedily to 42.

Both sides lost heavily, but Gould was still intrenched in the Erie. A suit was now commenced against Belmont and others for the purpose of showing that the suit recently instituted by the latter was not brought in good faith. Moreover, Gould's position was further strengthened through the action of a complacent judge, Blatchford by name. On the petition of a holder of recently issued stock, who "feared that the issue might be declared illegal," this magistrate directed $8,000,000 of the money of the company to be placed in the hands of the receiver (Gould), as a protection to the holders of such stock.[32]

About this time Gould was confronted by a rival receiver, appointed by a hostile judge. But Fisk and he fortified themselves within their headquarters, and, in the face of conflicting judicial orders, managed to maintain their hold on the Erie. Eventually their opponents gave up the hopeless contest; truce was established; and Gould was left to enjoy his receivership. When that was vacated, he once more assumed the Presidency of the road, from which position he was not deposed till March, 1872. Even then he re-

[32]*Commercial and Financial Chronicle,* November 21, 1868, Vol, VII, pp. 647, 648, 677.

mained director of the road for a time, and it was reported that his loss of position was solaced by a gift of $1,000,000, in repayment of advances and loans negotiated entirely on his own responsibility.[33]

During the period of his administration, the capital stock of the road had been increased $61,-425,700, and the "construction" account had risen from $49,247,700 in 1867 to $108,807,687.[34] Stock to the amount of $40,700,000 had been marketed by the firm of Smith, Gould, and Martin, and, incredible as it may seem, its sale had netted the company only $12,803,059. In the face of such proceedings, it is small wonder that the Erie was left to fall into a state of chronic bankruptcy, and to operate as a disturbing factor in the railroad world down to the present day.

Yet, after all, the movement to oust Gould

---

[33]*Commercial and Financial Chronicle,* March 16, 1872, Vol. XIV, p. 342.

[34]The New York *Times,* December 3, 1892.

Testimony was taken by the Hepburn Committee, in 1879, Vol. V., p. 18, to the effect that the road and equipment of the Erie could be replaced for about $40,000,000. It was also stated that the company's report to the State Engineer in 1873 showed under the head of "construction account," $47,000,000, representing a "discount on the sale of convertible bonds." It is also interesting to know that "legal expenses" of more than $890,000 were charged to the construction account in 1870. The witness furnishing this testimony had just been employed in taking an inventory of the road, and he had come to the conclusion "that the construction account not only covers the proper cost of the road, but, like charity, it covers a multitude of sins."

does not appear to have been the result of any aroused public sentiment. In fact, the public mind was firmly fixed on the desirability of preventing a coalition between the Erie and the New York Central. Gould even posed in the light of a public benefactor—the friend of the people and of the shipping public. He was the man who had circumvented the formation of a great monopoly. Just so had he been the disinterested friend of the farmer during his campaign to "bull" the gold market.

The effective opposition to the Gould management came seemingly from a group of speculative English holders of the Erie stock, who hoped to profit by the rise sure to follow his deposition.[35] Having succeeded in dislodging Gould from the Presidency, his opponents proceeded to take further measures. In July, 1872, suit was brought against him in the Court of Common Pleas (New York), to recover a sum of nearly $10,000,000, said to have been misappropriated by him, while an officer of the company. At the election held in the same month under an act of the New York Assembly, his connection with the company was entirely severed.[36] The following December, Gould undertook to convey to the

---

[35]*Commercial and Financial Chronicle*, March 30, 1872, Vol. XIV, p. 406.

Erie real estate and securities, having a (nominal) value of $9,086,000, in settlement of the claims against him.[37] Naturally, the stock rose when Gould's intentions became known, and suspiciously large amounts were offered for sale. Then came a distressing slump, when it began to be rumored that Gould's restitution had been largely a restitution in name. There was room for believing that he had again profited by his own misdeeds—that "buying at the bottom (he) had sold twice as much at the top," and had fulfilled his contracts after the drop in prices. It was estimated that he acquired several millions as the result of this, his farewell operation in Erie stocks.

II.

The West has always been the great field for the speculator. It is the land of big enterprises prematurely developed—a land in which the pioneers in investment are not so apt to profit, as to lay the foundations of a fortune for their immediate successors. At the period when Gould severed his relations with the Erie, the railroads of the West had just come into being, under the impetus of state and national loans and

---

[36]*Ibid.,* July, 1872.

[37]*Commercial and Financial Chronicle,* December 21, 1872, Vol, XV, p. 830. New York *Times,* December 3, 1892,

land grants. Needless to say, some of their pro-
moters had already become involved in difficulties. The Union Pacific, for example, was in
hard straits. It had been built "when the price
of labor and material was extremely high, government bonds at a discount, gold at a premium,
the national currency inflated," and no other
road within one hundred miles.[38] Moreover, the
method of financing its construction had been
peculiar, and, when completed, it was saddled
with interest payments on $27,000,000 first mort-
gage bonds, $27,000,000 government bonds, $10,-
000,000 income bonds, $10,000,000 land grant
bonds, and, if anything were left, dividend payments on $36,000,000 of stock. Surely, the fu-
ture did not appear altogether bright, and the
disclosures connected with the Credit Mobilier
Company[39]—the disgrace and death of Oakes
Ames—were further demoralizing to the good repute of the road. Following these revelations,
the Ames' stockholdings were thrown on the
market for what they would bring. Gould was
not slow to take advantage of this favorable opportunity to invest, and the purchases then made
laid the basis of his subsequent large interests in

---

[38]John P. Davis, *The Union Pacific Railway* (1894), p. 173.

[39]Credit Mobilier Investigation, House Report, No. 78, 42nd
Congress, 3rd Session, Feb. 18, 1873.

the Union Pacific.[40]   In the previous year, a
coterie headed by Vanderbilt's son-in-law, Horace F. Clark, had purchased control of the road,[41]
with a view to throwing its traffic over the New
York Central lines.   However, Clark's death in
1873 caused his holdings to be offered for sale,
and they were bought in by Gould at 35.   During this year alone Gould obtained 100,000 shares
of Union Pacific stock, doubling his holdings in
the course of the next five years.

Unhappily, the road was overburdened with
debt; the outlook was unpromising, and the price
of the stock soon fell to 14.   Something must be
done to rehabilitate it, or, at any rate, to make
its stock salable.   As the surest means to this
end, Gould advocated the policy of liberal dividend payments.   From July, 1875, to January,
1880, dividends to the amount of $11,900,000
were disbursed.[42]   The business of the road had
increased, to be sure, rising from $7,600,000 in
1870 to $13,200,000 in 1880, while the operating
expenses had decreased from 61.34 per cent. of
the gross earnings to 41.48 per cent.   However,

---

[40]Pacific Railway Commission; testimony of Charles Francis
Adams, Vol. I, p. 71.

[41]Henry K. White, *History of the Union Pacific Railway*
(1895), p. 55.
    Cf. *Poor's Manual of Railroads* for list of directors.

[42]White, *History of the Union Pacific Railway*, p. 60.

items were charged to the construction account,
which should have been accredited to operating
expenses, while, at the same time, the unusually
high passenger and freight rates that prevailed
during the period, helped to swell the gross earnings.[43]   Moreover, the interest on the debt, accruing to the United States, was excluded from
the income account, in accordance with a decision
of the courts that such interest was not payable
until the maturity of the bonds.   Nevertheless,
a failure to provide for these interest payments
meant eventual bankruptcy for the Union Pacific.   Meantime, dividend payments raised the
price of the stock, and enabled Gould gradually
to dispose of his holdings, until, by the end of
1879, he owned but 27,000 shares, out of a former maximum of 200,000.[44]

As he withdrew from the Union Pacific, Gould
began to invest in various bankrupt roads, of no
importance in themselves, but valuable in that
they enabled him to levy tribute on the Union Pacific.   His connection with the Kansas Pacific
and the Denver Pacific dates from 1875.   Both
companies were insolvent, and the value attach-

---

[43] Report of the Pacific Railway Commission, p. 53.

[44] Pacific Railway Commission; testimony of Addison Cam-
mack, Vol. I, p. 281.   He states that Gould sold to a syndicate
70,000 shares of stock of the Union Pacific some time before
March, 1879, the price of the sale being between 65 and 70.

ing to the Denver Pacific stock was altogether
contingent upon the value that Gould might be
able to infuse into the Kansas Pacific securities
(the Denver Pacific being the connecting link
between the Union Pacific and the Kansas Pacific). In 1877, the Kansas Pacific, in an en-
deavor to prevent foreclosure, issued a funded
mortgage of $15,000,000. At the time, it held
over 29,000 shares of the stock of the Denver
Pacific, received in payment of advances made to
the latter road. This stock was therefore used as
part security for the funding bonds. The desperate condition of the road enabled Gould and
his Union Pacific *confreres* to purchase largely
of its securities at very low prices, and, by 1879,
Gould himself had attained to a position of control.

He now disclosed to the astonished directors
of the Union Pacific a plan he had matured for
effecting the consolidation of the Union Pacific,
Kansas Pacific, and Denver Pacific roads—the
stock of all these companies to be exchanged
share for share for stock of the new combined
organization. By means of judicious dividend
payments, the stock of the Union Pacific had acquired a very fair reputation as an investment security, and the indignant directors (who hap-
pened to be more largely interested in the Union

Pacific than in either of the other roads) promptly rejected the proposition.[45]

Gould, without more ado, went to Kansas,
bought up the Missouri Pacific, which extended
from St. Louis to Kansas City, for $3,000,000,
and, as part of the transaction, purchased a controlling interest in the Kansas Central.   His
method of obtaining the Missouri Pacific was
characteristic.   He simply threatened to build
the Kansas Pacific as far east as the Missouri
Pacific built west, at the same time accompanying
the threat with an offer to purchase.[46] A few
days prior to this transaction, Gould had ob-

---

[45]Report of the Pacific Railway Commission, Vol. I, p. 58.
The relative standing of the three companies is shown as follows:

	Annual net earnings per mile, 1870-80.	Annual net interest per mile, 1870-80.
Union Pacific	$5,616.66	$3,185.39
Kansas Pacific	1,601.77	2,294.71
Denver Pacific	1,322.70	1,794.89

The stock held by Gould and other Union Pacific directors in
the Kansas Pacific at the time of the consolidation:

Jay Gould	$4,000,000
F. G. Dexter	125,700
E. H. Baker	27,400
Russell Sage	443,000
Elisha Atkins	45,600
F. L. Ames	179,600
Sidney Dillon	305,900

All of these men held large amounts of the consolidated bonds
and other securities of the Kansas Pacific and branch lines.

[46]White, *History of the Union Pacific Railway*, pp. 58, 59.
Pacific Railway Commission; testimony of Gould, Vol. I, p. 509.

tained 7,616 shares of stock of the Central Branch
of the Union Pacific, paying the extraordinary
price of $238 per share for securities which had
sold at $10 within the year.[47] However, control
of this road was for the moment essential to
Gould's plans; when he no longer needed it, he
graciously disposed of it to the Union Pacific for
exactly the sum that it cost him.

Thereafter Gould let it be known that his
views were altered. He would construct a Pacific road of his own by extending the Kansas
Pacific through Loveland Pass to Salt Lake City
and then to San Francisco, by means of the Central Pacific. This announcement frightened the
unhappy directors of the Union Pacific into com-
pliance with his original proposal, Gould all the
while protesting that the consolidation was not
so greatly to his advantage as his new scheme.
The three roads, that is, the Union Pacific, Denver Pacific, and Kansas Pacific, were merged
(January, 1880), the shares being exchanged for
new stock, dollar for dollar, the bonded indebtedness being left undisturbed. Of this new stock,
Gould received approximately 99,000 shares,
much of which was speedily disposed of, Gould
admitting that his desire to sell had been stimu-

---

[47]Report of the Pacific Railway Commission, p. 60.

lated by the fact that the consolidation had caused an advance of 30 points in stock quotations.[48]

It was generally conceded that the union of the three roads was advantageous, however hard the terms; and testimony was unanimous in favor of the branch line system advocated by Gould, who profited by buying up numerous little roads, and selling them to the Union Pacific at enhanced prices. No doubt, these acquisitions sometimes benefited the main line,[49] but it would seem that Gould in his fiduciary position should have confined his activity to suggesting such purchases to the management.

By 1883, Gould had entirely disposed of his interests in the Union Pacific, and that most opportunely. The past four years had been prosperous, but he was too shrewd a man not to take heed when disaster was approaching. Perhaps he saw it the more clearly, because he usually helped to precipitate it. At any rate, the competition of new lines that were building, as well as the heedless squandering of substance on branch roads

---

[48] Pacific Railway Commission; testimony of Jay Gould, Vol. I, p. 559. It is stated that Gould obtained his Kansas Pacific stock at 12½.

[49] However, the statement is made in the Report of the Pacific Railway Commission, Vol. I, p. 66, that the three branches (the Denver, South Park and Pacific Railway Company, the Central Branch Union Pacific, and the Kansas Central) "were all bought from Mr. Gould, and the terms at which they were acquired were such as to make it impossible to avoid a disastrous result."

and on dividend payments had reduced the Union Pacific to the verge of bankruptcy. When the deluded Charles Francis Adams became President in 1884, he found a floating debt of $10,-000,000 which had been allowed to accumulate, while Gould, under cover of dividend payments, unostentatiously disposed of his stock. But that was not all. As Adams plaintively remarked to the investigating committee of 1887, "In 1883 everything came on the Union Pacific at once. Before that time it was earning enormously" (Gould evidently induced him to believe that it was), "but at that time the Northern Pacific was completed through, which affected us very severely on Pacific Coast business, and on Montana business very severely indeed. The Denver and Rio Grande was completed through to Ogden, which affected us on business to Salt Lake. At the same time the Southern Pacific was completed through, which affected us on business to San Francisco and the Pacific. And almost at the same time the Horn Silver Mines ceased to be productive. The result was that our business fell off, if I recollect right, $4,000,000 in one year. At the same time our rates were reduced, and our expenses were necessarily increased."[50]

---

[50]Pacific Railway Commission; testimony of Charles Francis Adams, Vol. I, p. 85.

Adams at once introduced a policy of retrenchment—$16,000,000 was put into the property, one-half raised from the net revenues, while the stockholders went without dividends, the other half, from the sales of securities in the treasury. But the debt of the road continued to increase, and Gould, who had found it financially embarrassed, now left it in straits. His experience with the Erie had been repeated in certain respects, although his career had not been so spectacular. In both cases, he had profited as an individual; as for the roads, that is another story. Later he was to return and tender an unavailing succor to the Union Pacific,[51] but meantime his interests had veered in another direction, and he was busied in organizing an elaborate system of railroads in the southwest.

Gould secured an interest in the Wabash, St. Louis, and Pacific in 1879,[52] about the time that

---

[51] When the Adams management became hopelessly involved, Gould and Sage came to its assistance with loans. A large part of the floating debt was controlled by them, and, at the end of 1890, they took charge of the property, retired Adams and installed Sidney Dillon in the Presidency. In August, 1891, Gould contributed $5,000,000 to a syndicate formed to guarantee the floating debt, which, by that time, had attained enormous proportions. However, there was little to be got out of a continued active connection with the road. Its fate was clear to the most optimistic, and it was known several months before Gould's death that he was to withdraw from all participation in its concerns. Cf. Bradstreet's, Vol. XVIII, p. 760; Vol. XIX, pp. 66, 516; Vol. XX, p. 261.

[52] For the details which follow cf. *Poor's Manuals* for the period and the *Commercial and Financial Chronicle*.

he bought control of the Missouri Pacific. In the same year, he became a director of the Denver and Rio Grande, then in process of building. Early in 1880, he, together with certain other directors of the Union Pacific, appeared on the board of the Texas and Pacific.[53] After a struggle for control, he also forced his way into the Missouri, Kansas and Texas, whither he was again followed by the ubiquitous Union Pacific directors.[54] But his purchases did not stop there. In December, 1880, he secured a majority interest in the International and Great Northern, and, about the same time, he bought 70,000 shares of the stock of the St. Louis, Iron Mountain and Southern. It was conjectured that 40,000 shares of the stock of this latter road were obtained for somewhat less than $2,000,000[55]—a sum by no means small, however, in view of the fact that the road showed a deficit of more than $180,000 for the preceding year. During this period, Gould also undertook to build a new road, the New York, Lackawanna and Western, having

[53]The Texas and Pacific went into the hands of receivers in 1885. After being sold under foreclosure proceedings in 1887, Gould still remained in possession, and held the Presidency at the time of his death.

[54]This company was bankrupt at the time when Gould acquired control.

[55]*Commercial and Financial Chronicle,* December 18, 1880, Vol. XXXI, p. 653.

previously secured the co-operation of capitalists interested in the Delaware, Lackawanna and
Western. This last-named project was part of
an elaborate scheme to provide an eastern outlet
for the Wabash by means of the Great Western
of Canada and the Delaware, Lackawanna and
Western.

Having thus provided for his eastern connections, and having secured a firm hold on the
southwestern traffic situation, Gould proceeded
to carry out his plans of organization. The
Missouri Pacific was consolidated with the St.
Louis and Lexington, the Kansas City and
Eastern, the Lexington and Southern, the St.
Louis, Kansas, and Arizona, the Missouri River,
and the Leavenworth, Atchison, and Northwestern railroads.[56] In accordance with his customary
methods, Gould made this consolidation the occasion for an increased stock issue of $12,419,-
800. In December, 1880, the Missouri,
Kansas, and Texas was leased to the Missouri Pacific, the rental to be the net earnings of
the leased line.[57] In 1881, the Missouri Pacific

---

[56]*Ibid.*, August 21, 1880, Vol. XXXI, p. 205.

[57]The lease was abrogated in 1888, the accrued interest in excess of the surplus earnings being larger than the amount that
could be advanced by the Missouri Pacific under the terms of
the lease. From January 1st to June 30th, 1891, the road was in
the hands of a receiver, and the net earnings had to be applied
to repairs of the property.

acquired the ownership of the St. Louis, Iron Mountain, and Southern by giving three shares of its stock for four of the latter road. In March, the stockholders of this road had voted a $2,000,-000 bond increase, and had authorized an addition to its capital stock of $12,000,000, all this being done in view of the fact that the company had been unable the preceding year to meet the interest on its first and second income bonds. In accordance with the plan for a general union, the International and Great Northern was taken over by the Missouri, Kansas, and Texas, the exchange of stock being at the rate of two to one in favor of the latter road. The International and Great Northern ran through Central Texas, and was a very important adjunct of the Missouri Pacific, which thereby secured an outlet to the Gulf. However, in the usual fashion of the mismanaged, debt-burdened Gould properties, it defaulted in its interest payments several years later, and the lease was abrogated.

While all this was in progress, the Wabash had entered upon a career of positively voracious expansion. In 1880, a new $50,000,000 mortgage had been authorized[58] to furnish the wherewithal for retiring certain bonds, for building new lines,

---

[58] Only $17,000,000 of this new mortgage was issued.

for buying bridges and barges.   The next year,
the Wabash entered into an agreement with the
Central of New Jersey[59] and with the Pennsylvania, whereby the latter agreed to transmit
freight, delivered to it by the Central, over its
own lines, to the Wabash at Red Bank.[60]   Notwithstanding all these elaborate schemes for an

---

[59]The history of Gould's later connection with the Central of
New Jersey is typically interesting.   President Gowen of the
Baltimore and Ohio thought the Central would give his road an
excellent outlet to New York, and as Gould manifested no concern whatever, he proceeded, with the aid of the Vanderbilts, to
purchase control.   The Reading and the Baltimore and Ohio in
concert secured 92,000 shares of stock, and the directors in power
in the Central were thereupon confidently requested to resign.
The sole reply to this demand came in the form of a bill, which
Gould with the assistance of the Pennsylvania Railroad lobby
succeeded in rushing through the New Jersey legislature.   This
bill authorized the Central to increase its capital stock to an
amount necessary to pay off a bonded indebtedness of $8,000,000,
which was payable on demand.   This meant a possible stock issue
of 80,000 shares, of which the Baltimore and Ohio-Reading crowd
would be forced to purchase over 40,000 in order to retain control.
Truly, the days of the Erie had not been forgotten!   A suit was
promptly begun to estop the new issue, on the ground that the
charter provisions of the road forbade such an increase in its
capital stock without the consent of two-thirds of the stockholders.   A temporary injunction was granted, and was still in force,
when the time for a new election arrived.   The board decided not
to call a meeting.   Their opponents, relying upon an old New
Jersey statute, which provided that, where the directors failed to
call an annual meeting, it could be called by any five stockholders
by giving ten days' public advertisement, proceeded to call a
meeting for May 5th, 1882.   The Chancellor granted an order
forbidding an election at the time set, but finally fixed a day in
June for a new election—the first one held in eight years!   Thus
Gowen finally succeeded in securing a victory over Gould.
     Cf. *Commercial and Financial Chronicle,* Vol. XXXIV.

[60]The Wabash was preparing to extend its line to this point.
In 1882, the New York, Lackawanna and Western was leased in
perpetuity to the Delaware, Lackawanna and Western.   The ques-

extension of its operations, the Wabash passed the dividend on its preferred stock the very next year. Small wonder, when the company had assumed the obligations of all the miserably equipped little roads in its vicinity! A part of the January interest, moreover, was only met by taking up and selling some bonds on which a loan had previously been negotiated. In April, 1883, the Wabash was leased to another Gould property, the St. Louis, Iron Mountain, and Southern, the rental to be its net earnings. The reason for such an apparently perfunctory transaction is probably explained by a statement which appeared in the *Commercial and Financial Chronicle* at the time.[61] A guess was hazarded that Gould found it necessary to retain the Wabash in order to prevent the injury to the Missouri Pacific which would result from its going into the hands of a receiver. By leasing the road to one of his own lines for its net earnings simply, he ran no risks, and he was relieved of the necessity of carrying the stock to keep control, and of making continual advances to the company.

---

tion of an eastern outlet for the Wabash became once more a problem—one which George Gould has been attempting to solve at the present day by purchases of certain small eastern lines.

[61]*Commercial and Financial Chronicle,* April 21, 1883, Vol. XXXVI, p. 439.

However, it cannot be said that Gould assumed any chances of loss in making loans to
bankrupt corporations. He had means of pro-
tecting himself, not vouchsafed to the ordinary
bondholder or stockholder. For instance, when
the Wabash finally defaulted in the interest on its
general mortgage bonds, in 1884, the notes given
by Gould, Sage and Humphreys to take up its
floating debt were speedily protected by the issu-
ance of receivers' certificates in exchange for
them. A rather acrid, but, no doubt, approximately correct review of Gould's conduct of this
unwieldy company appeared in the *Commercial
and Financial Chronicle* shortly after the road
had been precipitated into bankruptcy. "Among
all Mr. Gould's railroad operations, none has
been more striking than that in connection with
Wabash. How the company was raised from
deep insolvency; how Cyrus W. Field allowed
himself to be made President for a time; how
stock was bought up at almost nothing and sold
out at fabulous prices; how the leases of innumerable lateral roads were made at immense rent-
als; how stock was listed in London; how the
general or blanket mortgage bonds were created
and widely distributed to the amount of $17,-
000,000, furnishing the required cash for a season; how the famous dividend of November,

1881, was declared on the preferred stock, when the company was already known to have a large deficit; the unloading of insiders on the strength of that dividend; the leasing of the Wabash to the St. Louis and Iron Mountain Railroad, giving control of the road without the ownership of a share of stock; the advance of money by directors; the collateral trust loan—the *dernier ressort* of modern railroad financiers; the final insolvency in June, 1884, and the appointment of one of the most prominent directors, a receiver; the issue of receivers' certificates to pay off notes endorsed by directors; the recent meeting in the nature of a funeral, at which Mr. Gould as President showed his resignation (controlling, with the Iron Mountain, the chief assets of the deceased), and the managers' committee submitted their plan for the future resurrection, in which the unprofitable leases made by them are to be shaken off, the lien of the general mortgage extinguished, the stockholders heavily assessed, and the directors are to be paid in cash—all the above circumstances contribute to make the history of Wabash, since Mr. Gould took it, one of the most remarkable and interesting that has ever occurred in American railroading. It is even phenomenal, embracing in a comparatively short period every phase of kite-flying, watering, stock-

jobbing, bankruptcy of the company and assessment of its stockholders, which are so frequently
commented on in London and Amsterdam, as
being the common characteristics of American
railroad management." [62]

With the purchase of a large interest in the St.
Louis and San Francisco, in January, 1882,
Gould secured control of all the roads leading
into the southwest, save the Atchison, Topeka
and Santa Fe. South of Kansas City and the
Missouri River and east and south of Kansas,
he had no competitors. The potential prosperity
of an immense area was in great part at his disposal. The history of railroad management in
the southwest became henceforth a history of his
activities, and it does not speak well for him that
that history should have been a dreary recital of
bankruptcies, receiverships, and foreclosures.

III.

Apart from his railway holdings, Gould had
but two large interests, and those were both in
great public service corporations, connected with
transportation—the Western Union Telegraph
Company, and the Manhattan Elevated Railway
Company. Gould early attempted to "break

---

[62]*Commercial and Financial Chronicle*, August 16, 1884, Vol.
XXXIX, p. 183.

into" the former, nor was he at all discouraged by
the fact that the Vanderbilts were apparently in
full control.   There were other ways of securing
an interest besides making direct stock purchases,
and he was prepared to use those means without
delay.   As a first step toward the realization of
his plans, he arranged to have himself and certain
other directors of the Union Pacific declared trus-
tees of the Atlantic and Pacific Telegraph Company—an unpromising concern, indeed, but one
well adapted to annoy the Western Union.   It
was announced, in June, 1874, that the contract
of the Union Pacific with the latter company had
been abrogated, and it was stated, furthermore,
that the Atlantic and Pacific would thereafter
compete for the California business.   Moreover,
the Atlantic and Pacific was about to construct
an independent line from Omaha to Chicago,
and it would soon have a system stretching from
ocean to ocean.   Notwithstanding these ambi-
tious schemes, the company exhibited a deficit of
$9,572 for the next year, but the management,
by no means discouraged, authorized an increase
of $5,000,000 in its capital stock, to be issued
at 20.

Meanwhile, the Atlantic and Pacific steadily
cut rates, and speculation was rife, as to what
action would be taken by the Western Union.   It

was soon evident; in 1887, the companies agreed to pool their gross receipts, upon a basis of division highly favorable to the Atlantic and Pacific.[63]   Subsequent to this arrangement, 429 offices of the latter corporation were closed, and its reduced business made necessary a payment of $40,000 by the Western Union to make up its stipulated percentage quota of the gross receipts.

Truly the bargain was not a bad one for Gould! But he was not satisfied, and, assuming control of a new concern, the American Union Telegraph Company, he harassed the Western Union more than ever.   Coming forward once again in the guise of a public benefactor, he let it be known that the American Union was designed to frustrate the unlawful operations of such a powerful, grasping corporation as the Western Union. The public was invited to look on approvingly, while the American Union busily extended its network of wires.   By January, 1880, 40,000 miles of line had been secured, and in the following July, another 12,000 miles were acquired, through the lease of the Dominion Telegraph Company of Canada.   Radical rate reductions, varying from

---

[63]Eighty-one and one-half per cent. of the gross earnings were to go to the Western Union; 12½ per cent., to the Atlantic and Pacific.   Moreover, the Western Union agreed to purchase 72,502 shares of the Atlantic and Pacific (over half its capital stock) at 25, giving 12,500 shares of the Western Union and $912,550 in cash, in return.

15 to 30 per cent., were instituted, and altogether, considering the patronage which Gould, as a great railroad magnate, could give to his new creation, the outlook seemed decidedly serious for the older company. The inevitable result was a consolidation, which was brought about in 1881.[64] Gould and his allies thereupon assumed a position of dominance in the new Western Union, and at the time of Gould's death in 1892, the President of the company estimated his stock-holdings at $20,000,000.

Gould believed in the earning powers of the Manhattan Elevated just as he believed in those of the Western Union, and, once in control, he did not display his usual readiness to dispose of its stock. However, the way to power was, in the first place, devious, though profitable. The Manhattan Company had been organized solely for the purpose of leasing the New York and the Metropolitan Elevated railroads. It had guaranteed a ten per cent. dividend on the stock of both these roads, as a condition of the lease, and

[64]The American Union received 150,000 shares of the Western Union for 100,000 shares of stock and $5,000,000 of bonds of the new company. The Atlantic and Pacific, which also entered the consolidation, obtained 84,000 shares in exchange for 140,000 of its own shares. The Western Union, at the same time, increased its capital stock $38,926,590, of which $15,526,590 went to the stockholders of the original company, representing additions to construction, made since 1866.

it had at the same time issued $13,000,000 of its own stock, which represented nothing so far as could be seen but its capitalized expectations of profit. Suits were at once begun by dissatisfied stockholders of the underlying properties, asking a dissolution of the new holding company. It became involved in all sorts of financial difficulties, and annoying litigation, which caused its stock to decline rapidly in value. The New York *World* (Gould's newspaper) published the gloomiest accounts concerning the Manhattan's probable future.[65]   Its stock finally descended to 26 1-2; and the men in control began to sell heavily. About this time, it first began to be rumored that Gould was taking all the securities offered at these low prices,[66] the stories published in his newspaper having, strangely enough, no power to terrify him.

Meanwhile, as a result of the various suits which had been instituted against the company, receivers were finally appointed—Judge John F. Dillon and Albert C. Hopkins, both trusted lieutenants of Jay Gould.[67] The latter had been busily engaged in buying Manhattan stock for some time past, and he is said to have purchased

---

[65] New York *Times,* December 3, 1892.
[66] *Railroad Gazette,* June 17, 1881.
[67] *Ibid.,* July 15, 1881.

70,000 shares at prices ranging from 16 to 20.[68]
Eventually, all the pending suits were called off,
and a settlement was effected between the Manhattan and the two other companies.   When
Gould became President of the reorganized combination in November, 1881, the stock, which had
sold down to 16, was being quoted at 55.   There
was much grumbling about the mysterious fashion in which many troublesome suits had been
quietly set aside, but there was nothing to be
done.   Gould, securely installed, was not to be
lightly displaced, once he had made up his mind
to stay.

With the account just given, the tale of
Gould's numerous activities has by no means
been told, but the most important phases of his
business career have been briefly recounted.   In
view of the number and variety of his interests,
the diversity of the sources from which he drew
his profits, it is significant, above all, to know that
he had faith in\but three of the corporations with
which he was connected, as long-time paying investments—the Missouri Pacific, the Western
Union, and the Manhattan Elevated.   There is
need, perhaps, of no other commentary than this,
to show the highly speculative character of the
greater part of the gains amassed by him during
the course of his lifetime.

---

[68] New York *Times,* Dec. 3, 1892.

CHAPTER IV.

GROUP FORTUNES:

THE "STANDARD OIL" AND THE "MORGAN" MEN.

AT the beginning of the seventies, a condition of indiscriminate competition prevailed within the petroleum refining industry, and gave impetus to the movement, initiated by John D. Rockefeller, which early made for the union of the large interests composing what came to be known as the Standard Oil Alliance.[1] By the close of the decade this Alliance was the most effective and powerful of all the industrial organizations that had come into being, and when the trust succeeded the looser, extra-legal combination in 1882, it had an estimated capital of $70,000,000, of which the pipe-line interests were said to have constituted about one-third.

---

[1] The working arrangements of the "alliance" were close and effective because of the fact that the stock ownership of the various companies composing it was distributed in such a way as to make the advantage of one member of the organization more or less the advantage of all. In other words, the device of a "community of interests" was employed, with such good results, moreover, that by 1879 the association included from 90 to 95 per cent. of the refining interests of the country, besides having control of all the principal pipe lines for the transportation of oil.

Cf. Ida M. Tarbell, *The History of the Standard Oil Company.*

The early history of the methods whereby the
Oil Trust, under the leadership of John D.
Rockefeller, grew and prospered, is sufficiently
familiar to need no elaboration. Having successfully applied his energy and organizing ability
to the establishment of his private business, Mr.
Rockefeller then turned his attention to the development of the trust. The conditions of the
time, the policy of the railroads, immensely aided
the task of amalgamation. As always, the alliance of transportation with trading and industrial interests gave a superiority within the competitive field out of all proportion to technical or
personal advantages, although those were undoubtedly great. Indeed, it is not always easy
to see to what extent the immense gains of the
"trust" were the result of more economical and
better methods of production—to what extent
they were due to competitively cheaper methods
of marketing, an outgrowth of the peculiarly
intimate relations maintained with the railroads,
and, later, of the advantages due to the ownership of an elaborate pipe-line system. But this
much may be conceded: however persuasive Mr.
Rockefeller may have been, he must needs have
acquired control of a concern boasting some degree of effectiveness before he could demand special consideration from the railroads, even in

those days of unlicensed competition. Nevertheless, such favors once obtained, the process of
growth was enormously facilitated, quite apart
from differences in personal shrewdness or improvements in technical processes. When, as in
this case of the Standard Oil Trust, extra-indus-
trial competitive advantages were combined with
technical superiority, immense gains were sure to
result and the process of monopolization was certain to continue.

By 1888, the trust was earning dividends of
from $16,000,000 to $20,000,000 on a capitaliza-
tion of $90,000,000; and, in view of these large
returns, it might have been expected that the investments of the men in control of the Standard
Oil properties would be found to be of considerable extent. But in point of fact, their outside
interests do not seem to have been of any great
importance prior to 1887 or 1888. Clearly, there
were no evidences of that unanimity of action in
the placing of investments which has later operated to make the so-called Standard Oil group
a power in the industrial and financial world at
large. Then they were pre-eminent in only one
field of activity—that of petroleum refining. The
explanation of this fact is not far to seek. In the
earlier days large dividend payments could be

very profitably reinvested in the business from which they were derived—in improvements in processes, in additions to holdings, and in the development of allied and subsidiary industries. The pipe-line system, for example, which had been so effectively extended, had required large expenditures for the purchase of competing lines and the building of new ones. The utilization of by-products, too, had been largely undertaken since 1875, while natural gas, being found in the neighborhood of the oil fields and requiring similar methods of piping and drilling, offered another obvious avenue of investment. But, although with this growth in size and comprehensiveness, and with increased economies of production, dividends were becoming progressively larger, the opportunities for their reinvestment were none the less rapidly diminishing. A time must come when profits would grow to be sufficiently unwieldy to present a serious problem in investment, and that time seems to have been reached toward the close of the eighties.

All this does not mean that there had been no outside investments whatever prior to the period in question. Individual members of the Standard Oil Trust had without doubt been connected with other lines of activity, notably with the railroads of the country.[2] But none of these early investments are of particular importance as evidencing an extension of the group interests. They seem to have been purely personal matters, and as such they are significant only as indications of the probable direction to be taken by later and more important investments. As has been said, the period of general group expansion does not begin until 1887 or 1888. In the former year John D. Rockefeller became a member of the syndicate that bought out the Minnesota Iron Company.[3] Following the change of management, Benjamin Brewster and Henry M.

---

[2]For example, Henry M. Flagler appeared on the directorate of the Valley Railroad Company in 1879. In 1882 William Rockefeller became director of the Chicago, Milwaukee and St. Paul. Benjamin Brewster, a holder of Standard Oil certificates, was perhaps more especially a railroad man prior to 1881, when he became vice-president of the National Transit Company (the Standard Oil pipe-line organization). He had been interested in the construction of the Chicago, Rock Island and Pacific, becoming a director of the company in 1879 and continuing his connection with it until his death in 1897. Jabez A. Bostwick (onetime president of the American Transfer Company, and later trustee and treasurer of the Standard Oil Trust) also had large individual interests in railroads. In 1886, he became president of the New York and New England, and about the same time acquired stock holdings in other New England roads.

Concerning Brewster, cf. *Railway and Engineering Review*, Sept. 11, 1897, Vol. XXXVII, p. 530; concerning Bostwick, cf. *Railroad Gazette*, December 17, 1886; concerning Flagler's appearance on the directorate of the Valley Railroad, cf. *Poor's Manual*, 1879; concerning William Rockefeller, director of the Chicago, Milwaukee and St. Paul, cf. *Poor's Manual*, 1882.

[3]*Commercial and Financial Chronicle*, May 21, 1887, Vol. XLIV, p. 653.

Flagler were elected directors of the company as well as of its railroad, the Duluth and Iron Range, leaving no doubt that the "Standard" (to use the term in a newer, more detached sense) was interested.[4] About 1887, or somewhat later, Rockefeller interests appeared in the Northern Pacific and in the Missouri, Kansas and Texas,[5] while in 1888 William P. Thompson, C. W. Harkness, Charles Pratt, and Oliver H. Payne —all Standard Oil men in high standing—entered simultaneously the directorate of the Ohio River Railroad Company. Evidences of an organized expansion of investment interests are therefore not lacking to afford justification for dating the beginning of a second period of development from this time. During the new era Standard Oil holdings ceased to be regarded as trust stocks simply; they also included the outside investment interests of members of the group.

---

[4] *Poor's Manual of Railroads,* 1888.

[5] *Commercial and Financial Chronicle,* June 7, 1890, Vol. L, p. 801, says, "Parties familiar with the affairs of the company (i. e., the M. K. & T.) remark that the presence on the board of Mr. Freeman, Treasurer of the Standard Oil Company, and Mr. Colgate Hoyt, the Standard Oil representative in Northern Pacific, is a feature of the reorganization as accomplished. It emphasizes the fact that the Standard Oil people whom Mr. Enos has represented for over two years in his relations with the property continue to have a large and active interest in the road."

Notwithstanding the nature of the expansion that was taking place, the trust was nevertheless still recognized as the nucleus from which the larger, more exclusively financial alliance took its growth. Men interested directly in the Standard Oil Trust formed the Standard Oil group; and it was not until some years later, when this connection had become exceedingly attenuated, that the trust sank into a position of relative insignificance. Meanwhile the members of the group continued to augment their wealth and to add to the variety of their investment interests with a facility deserving of comment. It is true that the methods whereby large industrial concerns or single individuals compel or otherwise induce their weaker competitors to join with them or else be forced out of business have become fairly familiar from constant iteration. But less space has been given to discussion of the means by which a group of investors (dating their union from some enterprise undertaken in common) may further extend their control by proceeding against the property of unorganized alien interests. The more powerful the group and the greater its resources, the more numerous, of course, are its opportunities to gain by such operations. It may, perhaps, obtain a foothold in legitimate commercial fashion, by extending aid to the financially embarassed upon terms favorable to itself. Or it may increase its holdings by direct purchase, by gradual acquisition, or by other means.

A narration of the incidents leading up to the acquirement of control of certain Minnesota iron ore properties by the "Standard" affords an excellent illustration of the methods whereby this earlier extension of investment interests was profitably and easily effected. The owners of the Mountain Iron and Biwabik mines—two rich properties of the Mesaba range—had been engaged in building a railroad, the Duluth, Missabe, and Northern, from the mines to the lake.[6] Early in 1892 they became involved in financial difficulties, and at this juncture they were approached by an agent of Mr. Rockefeller, who offered them a loan of $1,600,000, in return for which the Duluth, Missabe, and Northern, and the mining companies owned by those interested in the road, were to contract to ship ore in the vessels of the American Steel Barge Company[7] for a number of years. The original bond issue of the road was also to be retired and a new issue

[6]Iron Age, January 7, 1892, Vol. XLIX, p. 16; also ibid., February 4, 1892, p. 198.

[7]The American Steel Barge Company was a Rockefeller property; cf. Iron Age, December 29, 1892, Vol. L, p. 1281,

8

of $2,000,000 to be put up as collateral for the loan.[8] Having quelled opposition to this plan by purchasing the interests of certain minority shareholders[9], the newly-formed syndicate proceeded to buy a number of valuable properties.[10] Early in 1893 rumors of a pending consolidation began to be rife. It was an especially propitious time to conduct negotiations aiming at the control or acquisition of mines. The panic of 1893 was on; ore producers were in desperate straits; mines were shutting down; loans on any terms were desired. The situation emphasized the advantage possessed by a wealthy group of investors with judiciously distributed holdings and well established banking connections. The men in control of the Duluth, Missabe, and Northern needed assistance, as did the rest of the mine owners. They therefore secured, through the vice-president of the American Steel Barge Company a loan of $432,575, for which they gave their notes secured by shares of stock of the Mountain Iron and the Missabe Iron companies,

---

[8]*Iron Age,* December 29, 1892, Vol. L, p. 1281; also *Iron Trade Review,* June 6, 1895, Vol. XXVIII.

[9]For mention of the controversy preceding a sale of minority interests, cf. *Iron Age,* February 2, 1893, Vol. LI, p. 249; *Railway Age,* February 10, 1893, Vol. XVIII, p. 123.

[10]*Iron Age,* March 16, 1893, Vol. LI, p. 622; *ibid.,* April 13, 1893, p. 858.

and the Duluth, Missabe, and Northern Rail-way.[11] It is highly probable, too, that direct loans were made them.[12] At any rate, it soon became evident that the transaction was but an-other step in the direction of an ultimate shifting of control.

In September, 1893, rumors of a pending con-solidation became justified by the formation of the Lake Superior Consolidated Iron Mines Company, which took over the majority interests of some ten or eleven Mesaba mines, the Duluth, Missabe, and Northern Railway (with its ore docks), and the Rockefeller interests on the Go-gebic range and in the Spanish-American mines of Cuba.[13]. The consolidation had been effected but a short time when it became evident that the original mine owners and railway projectors had been dispossessed of control. A series of dis-putes and litigations arose, some of the owners claiming that the stock offered as collateral for loans had been unlawfully disposed of;[14] others

---

[11]Cf. facts disclosed in suit of Merritt et al. vs. American Steel Barge Company, *Federal Reporter*, LXXIX, p. 228.

[12]New York *Tribune*, June 15, 1895.

[13]*Iron Age*, September 7, 1893, Vol. LII, p. 444.

[14]The Merritt brothers had contributed to the consolidation 51 per cent. of the share capital of the Mountain Iron, the Biwabik, and the Mesaba Mountain mines in addition to other properties (cf. *Iron Age*, July 21, 1893). In 1894 they brought suit against the American Steel Barge Company to recover the value of 13,313

asserting that their property had been taken over at unjustly low valuations, as the result of misrepresentation.[15] Matters were not completely adjusted until sometime in 1897. Meanwhile the company once within the control of wealthy

---

shares of stock in the recently formed Lake Superior Consolidated Iron Mines Company. The loan of $432,575 obtained from Wetmore (of which mention has been made) was secured by stocks of the Mountain Iron and Missabe Iron Companies, and the Duluth, Missabe and Northern Railway—which stocks were not to be repledged nor disposed of in any way. Wetmore, however, transferred all the railway stocks to Mr. Rockefeller—as a pledge for a debt, he said. The Merritts agreed to let this pass as a sale of stock for their benefit, although a short time before the same man had converted $90,000 worth of their bonds to his own use, upon which occasion they had elected to "waive the tort committed." It is no surprise, therefore, to learn that Wetmore later sold the promissory notes and the rest of the pledged stocks in his possession to the American Steel Barge Company, of which he was vice-president and managing officer. The stocks were subsequently converted into shares of the Lake Superior Consolidated Iron Mines Company. Upon maturity of the notes, the Barge Company brought suit in a New York court and secured a decision authorizing the sale of the notes and collateral, the latter being bought in by the company for $25,000. The Merritts had previously sued the Barge Company for the value of this collateral, but, the suit being brought in a Minnesota court, it was held that the decision of the New York court rendered first constituted a bar to action. Had the Merritts sued for the return of their stock, the Minnesota court, as having first jurisdiction, would have been entitled to retain it, since it would have been compelled to take possession of personal property. The decision of the United States Circuit Court was reaffirmed March 1, 1897, by the Circuit Court of Appeals.
   Cf. suit Merritt et al. vs. American Steel Barge Co., *Federal Reporter,* Vol. LXXV, p. 813; and Vol. LXXIX, p. 228.
   [15]Another suit afterward compromised was brought by the Merritts on the ground that the Spanish-American and Gogebic properties were taken into the consolidation at greatly inflated values.
   Cf. *Federal Reporter,* Vol. LXXVI, p. 909, Rockefeller vs. Merritt. For conjectures as to the terms of settlement, cf. *Iron Trade Review,* February 18, 1897; *Iron Trade Review,* March 4,

financiers rapidly acquired new mines both by lease and by purchase, while the Duluth, Missabe, and Northern soon had a practical monopoly of the ore transportation of the range.

The most important development, however, of the period under discussion lay not in the acquisition by the Standard Oil Group of valuable mining properties, but in the addition to its resources of substantial banking facilities. The alliance with the National City Bank had presumably been established by 1894, and although the bank was by no means in a position of such exceptional power as at present, its connections were nevertheless extensive.[16] Thus the members of the group found the process of fortune accumulation further facilitated, because of the ease

---

1897, Vol. XXX; New York *Tribune*, February 13, 1897. For details concerning the McKinley properties cf. *Iron Age*, June 22, 1893, Vol. LI, p. 387. Regarding controversies, cf. *Iron Age*, May 30, 1895, Vol. LV, p. 1136; *Iron Trade Review*, June 6, 1895; *ibid.*, June 13, 1895. Concerning "terms of settlement," cf. *ibid.*, August 15, 1895, Vol. XXVIII.

[16]It had a large representation in the United States Trust Company and in the Farmer's Loan and Trust Company. Its president, James Stillman, was a director of the New York Security and Trust Company, and two of its directors were also on the board of the Bank of the State of New York. Moreover, William Rockefeller was director both of the Hanover National Bank and of the Leather Manufacturers' National Bank. Other important financiers interested in the bank were connected with outside ventures, as for instance the Consolidated Gas Company, of which Percy R. Pyne (president of the National City, 1882-91), and Samuel Sloan (vice-president of the National City) had been directors since its formation in 1884. That the National City interests in this company in 1894 were quite heavy is evi-

with which credit accommodations could be secured in aid of new projects.

Sufficient evidence has now been adduced to make it apparent that by 1893 or 1894 Standard Oil had developed into an important investment power, controlling a vast amount of wealth. Standard Oil men had gained entrance into rich ore properties, such as the Minnesota Iron Company and the Lake Superior Consolidated Iron Mines Company. They were in western railroads, such as the Northern Pacific and the Missouri, Kansas, and Texas. They had holdings in eastern roads (the New York, New Haven and Hartford, the Ohio River Railroad Company, and the Delaware, Lackawanna and West-

---

denced by the fact that besides the two men just mentioned, Roswell G. Rolston, Moses Taylor Pyne, and James Stillman were on its directorate.

The National City contingent also figured prominently in railroads. Stillman had long been interested in western roads. He was director of the Chicago, Milwaukee and St. Paul from 1879 to 1889, and he had held a place on the directorates of several smaller railroads. In 1893 he became director of the Delaware, Lackawanna and Western, with which William Rockefeller had been connected since 1890, and of which Samuel Sloan was president at the time (1893). Moses Taylor, president of the National City from 1855 until his death in 1882, had been identified with the road during his lifetime. He had also been interested in the Western Union Telegraph Company, and the presence of Samuel Sloan and Percy R. Pyne on the directorate of the latter company in 1894 would indicate that the interest of the National City thus acquired had not been relinquished.

For facts concerning Moses Taylor, cf. *Rhodes' Journal of Banking,* May, 1882; *Bankers Magazine,* May, 1882; for the accession of Stillman to the presidency of the National City, see *Bankers Magazine,* December, 1891; cf. also lists of directors of *Poor's Manual of Railroads.*

ern). Some of the group were identified with the National Lead Company, successor to the Lead Trust, 1891; others, probably, with the American Cotton Oil Company.[17] Standard Oil men had acquired interests in street railway and electric-lighting properties, to wit, the North American Company;[18] and finally they were allied (more correctly, perhaps, identified) with the financial interests in control of the National City Bank and its affiliated institutions.

---

[17]The American Cotton Oil Trust was formed in 1884. It was generally believed at the time that it had Standard Oil men among its backers, although no substantial evidence was adduced to support such a belief. Cf. for instance, J. S. Jeans, *Trusts, Pools, and Corners,* Chap. VIII, p. 101. It is reasonably certain that Standard Oil men were interested in the National Lead Trust. Indeed, W. P. Thompson, at one time secretary of the Standard Oil Company of Ohio, became president of the Lead Trust about two years after its formation, at the solicitation, as he himself says, of Charles Pratt and H. H. Rogers. "In 1889 my friends, H. H. Rogers and the late Charles Pratt, both of whom had had large experience in the lead and paint business, knowing that I was about to retire from my association with the Standard Oil Company, called my attention to the fact that the National Lead Trust was desirous of my becoming interested with them." Cf. Depew, *One Hundred Years of American Commerce,* Vol. II, Chap. LXIV, p. 440, *The Lead Industry,* by William P. Thompson.

[18]The North American Company was originally intended to take over the assets of the Oregon and Transcontinental Company. It was later empowered to acquire stock of street railway and lighting properties. Charles L. Colby, the first vice-president of the company, had been frequently associated with Mr. Rockefeller; Colgate Hoyt, a member of the board of directors, represented the Rockefeller interests in the Northern Pacific; E. D. Bartlett was also a director.

Iron Age, April 13, 1893, Vol. LI, p. 858; cf. also *Commercial and Financial Chronicle,* November 15, 1890, Vol. LI, p. 680; *ibid.,* June 3, 1893, Vol. LVI, p. 931.

But the fact that the group had secured recognition as a force in the investment world at large did not mean that its evolution was complete. It was merely in a position to enter upon a new era of wealth expansion, furnishing some striking parallelisms with the early period, when members of the Standard Oil Trust were struggling to extend their hold on the petroleum-refining industry. Then, they had gained in wealth and power by allying themselves with their most important competitors in the field, and thus had come to enjoy all the profits incident to a monopoly. But the competitors in this more comprehensive struggle were not to be refiners of petroleum, but groups of financiers representing important and highly diversified industrial and financial interests. Competition among these groups was quite a different matter from competition within the limits of a single industry, covering as it did so wide an investment field. Obviously, when such opposing forces contended one against another, the results were certain to prove much more far-reaching than if the several group holdings had been confined to but one line of investment. Should "Standard Oil" secure a position of dominance among these competitive groups, what limits could be placed upon the possibilities of fortune getting held out to its members? They would then enjoy monopolistic advantages, not alone within a single industry, but over an immense field of trade and transportation.

It is, in fact, possible to trace the growth of a community of interests and to adduce certain facts which seem to indicate that this particular group, namely, the Standard Oil, may sometime come to dominate the entire investment field, as the smaller unit long ago came to control the industry of petroleum refining. First, however, it will be necessary to touch briefly upon certain facts relating to a number of the important groups of investors who were brought into relations with Standard Oil in the course of the next few years.

In 1893, a date which marks a turning point in the financial history of the country, the Goulds and the Vanderbilts were still in the ascendancy. The men in control of the Pennsylvania Railroad were also a force in the community, while Huntington in the Southern Pacific wielded a powerful one-man control. But all these interests, extensive though they might be, were more or less jealously confined to a single investment field— railroads. The Vanderbilt power was grounded almost exclusively upon its control of the New York Central and subsidiary lines. Outside of the Western Union Telegraph Company, the Goulds may be said to have had no important holdings in other than railroad securities. Harriman had not yet been spoken of in connection with Standard Oil, and the Moores were unknown save as organizers of the New York Biscuit and Diamond Match companies.[19] Morgan was still in a subordinate position as an ally of the Vanderbilts. In fact, the firm of Drexel, Morgan and Company, though well established and enjoying influential financial connections, had apparently been chiefly occupied up to that time with placing the investments of its rich clients. Nothing had been heard of the so-called Morgan railway systems, steamship lines, or steel trusts. But with the financial disturbances of 1893, which led to the bankruptcy of so many railroads, came the rise of the Morgan group as an independent investment power—a development almost spectacular in its suddenness.

The first of the railroad reorganizations undertaken by the firm was that of the Richmond and West Point Terminal Railway and Warehouse Company. In this case the security holders themselves made application to Drexel, Mor-

---

[19] For accounts of illegitimate speculation in the stocks of these companies carried on by the Moores, cf. *Commercial and Financial Chronicle,* August 29, 1896, and October 10, 1896.

gan and Company, who, after one refusal, at
length agreed early in 1893 to take charge of the
reorganization, upon assurances of a strict com-
pliance with their terms.[20] By the close of 1894
the new Southern Railway Company had been
established, to operate upon a more conservative
financial basis than its bankrupt predecessor.
The stock of the company was placed in the
hands of a voting trust consisting of J. P. Morgan, George F. Baker (president of the First
National Bank of New York), and Charles La-
nier,[21] while Messrs. Spencer, Wright and Coster, all of the firm of Drexel, Morgan and Company, were placed on the board of directors.[22]
The reorganization resulted in the Morgan interest being left in control of a road that later developed into one of the great railway systems of
the country.

In February, 1893, the Philadelphia and
Reading—the most important of the anthracite
coal roads—went into bankruptcy. It was reported that Morgan-Vanderbilt interests had secured control of the company, but this report

[20]*Bradstreet's,* April 22, 1893, Vol. XXI, p. 243; May 27, 1893;
Vol. XXI, p. 329.

[21]*Commercial and Financial Chronicle,* November 10, 1894,
Vol. LIX, p. 836.

[22]*Ibid.,* October 27, 1894, Vol. LIX, p. 739.

was vigorously denied at the time. Morgan, however, eventually undertook to adjust the finances of the road,[23] and it was thought that he, as well as others associated with him, secured large amounts of the stock and preference bonds thrown on the market by holders unwilling to pay the twenty per cent. assessment announced under the reorganization plan.[24]   The road was sold under foreclosure, September, 1896, together with the Philadelphia and Reading Coal and Iron Company, and was purchased by the reorganization committee for $20,500,000.[25]   When the reorganization was completed, the stock of the new Reading Company, which took over the securities of the older road and its subsidiary properties, was deposited with a voting trust consisting of J. P. Morgan, F. P. Olcott, president of the Central Trust Company, and one other selected by them. The first board of managers, moreover, contained three strong Morgan representatives.[26]

---

[23] *Bradstreet's,* July 13, 1895, Vol. XXIII, p. 437.

[24] *Bradstreet's,* December 21, 1895, Vol. XXIII, p. 805; cf. also *Poor's Manual of Railroads,* 1896, pp. 805, 806.

[25] *Commercial and Financial Chronicle,* September 26, 1896, Vol. LXIII, p. 560.

[26] C. H. Coster, F. L. Stetson, and George C. Thomas.   (Cf. *Poor's Manual of Railroads,* 1896 and 1897.)   In 1901 Morgan secured control of the Central of New Jersey and turned it over to the Reading, upon payment, it is said, of a most adequate compensation.   Cf. Report of the Industrial Commission, Vol. XIX, p. 461, 1902: "According to competent testimony before the

Similarly, the New York, Lake Erie and Western, which went into the hands of a receiver shortly after the Reading bankruptcy, came within Morgan's power,[27] as did the Hocking Valley, which defaulted in its interest payments in 1897.[28] Later in the same year Morgan's assistance was invoked again in behalf of the Lehigh Valley Railroad, as it was thought that, in view of the control he had come to exercise over certain coal roads, it would be to his interest to preserve the solvency of all of them.[29] However that may be, the banking house of J. P. Morgan

Industrial Commission, the price paid to the banking house of J. P. Morgan and Co., which secured control of the shares before selling them to the Reading Co., was the highest in the history of the Central Railroad of New Jersey."

[27]J. P. Morgan, Louis Fitzgerald, president of the Mercantile Trust Company, and Sir Charles Tennant, held the stock of the Erie in a voting trust, while Charles Coster, E. B. Thomas, Samuel Spencer, and F. L. Stetson were among the directors. The syndicate in charge of the reorganization agreed to provide $10,000,000 for assessments on all stock not assenting to the plan proposed and to take $15,000,000 new prior lien bonds. *Bradstreet's,* August 31, 1895.

[28]The Hocking Valley defaulted in the interest payments on its consolidated 5's, of which Mr. Morgan was said to have been the largest individual holder, although he also owned a considerable amount of preferred stock. Cf. *Commercial and Financial Chronicle,* February 20, 1897, Vol. LXIV; February 27, 1897, Vol. LXIV.

[29]Indeed, it was said at the time that through the absolute power of the Morgan interests in the Reading and the representation which allied financial powers (Standard Oil and Vanderbilt representatives?) had obtained in the Delaware and Hudson and the Delaware, Lackawanna, and Western, it was believed that fully 60 per cent. of the anthracite coal production of the country was in his hands. Cf. *Bradstreet's,* July 17, 1897, Vol. XXV, p. 453.

and Company agreed to adjust the finances of
the road[30]—a task which was successfully performed, and by the beginning of January, 1901,
Morgan men had come into undisputed control
of this company.[31]   Still another of the roads that
went under during the period from 1893 to 1897
came under the Morgan influence.   It was the
Northern Pacific, which became insolvent in
1893, but because of complications due to the
appointment of numerous receivers with conflicting duties, was not reorganized until 1896,
when the plan brought forward by J. P. Morgan and Company, with the co-operation of the
Deutsche Bank of Berlin, was successfully executed.[32]   As a result of his interest in the Northern Pacific, Morgan first came into relations with
James J. Hill, president of the Great Northern,
who was supposed to have bought largely of the
Northern Pacific securities the year before.[33]
The two roads under the leadership of Morgan
and Hill, respectively, thus came into harmonious

---

[30]*Commercial and Financial Chronicle,* March 13, 1897, Vol.
LXIV, p. 516.

[31]*Commercial and Financial Chronicle,* June 24, 1899, Vol.
LXVIII, p. 1226; January 12, 1901, Vol. LXXII, p. 87.

[32]*Poor's Manual of Railroads,* 1896.   The syndicate subscribed
$45,000,000 for the purpose of carrying the plan through and of
providing for working capital and improvements.

[33]*Commercial and Financial Chronicle,* May 18, 1895, Vol. LX,
p. 874.

relationship some time before the Northern Securities Company was formed.

By the end of 1897, as a result of the panic conditions of the preceding four years, Mr. Morgan together with his associates had succeeded in gaining a position of pre-eminence among the important railroad groups of the country. He either had control, or was in a fair way to gain control, of four important coal roads—the Reading, the Erie, the Lehigh, the Hocking Valley. He held chief place in the Southern Railway and in the Northern Pacific system; and he had come into amicable contact with James J. Hill, of the Great Northern.[34] A record such as this affords an excellent illustration of the ease with which powerful financiers (or individuals with powerful financial backing) can enlarge their holdings in time of crisis. Then it is that opportunities for investment abound, and large capitalists coming to the aid of the financially embarrassed may freely dictate their own terms, in many cases demanding a controlling interest in the companies requiring assistance.

---

[34]His railroad holdings have continued to enlarge since that time. The Southern Railway has made large additions to its mileage by the annexation of other roads. In 1902 Morgan came into control of the Louisville and Nashville, acquiring his interests from John W. Gates. *Bradstreet's*, October 4, 1902, Vol. XXX, p. 627.

While the Morgan group was striding so rapidly into prominence, Standard Oil had been
strengthening its hold on properties already acquired. It had also entered into important contracts with the Oliver Iron Mining Company,[35]
which was engaged in extensive operations on
the Mesaba; and it had materially extended its
gas interests, notably in the Brooklyn Union Gas
Company,[36] incorporated in 1895 for the purpose
of taking over control of the various gas companies of that city. The same period (1893-97)
saw the rise of another important group of financiers—the   Harriman-Kuhn-Loeb   syndicate,
which was soon to become generally recognized
as a part of the larger Standard Oil group.[37]
The syndicate first attracted public attention as
a result of its successful reorganization of the

[35] At that time five-sixths of the stock of the Oliver Iron
Mining Company was owned by the Carnegie Steel Company. Cf.
James H. Bridge, *History of the Carnegie Steel Company,* Chap.
XVII, pp. 258-60.

[36] *Commercial and Financial Chronicle,* June 15, 1895, Vol. LX,
p. 1057; ibid., Sept. 14, 1895, Vol. LXI, p. 473.

[37] Of the early history of this group I am ignorant. I have
seen a statement to the effect that its nucleus was the Illinois Central Railroad, of which Harriman had been a director since 1883.
Cf. *Commercial and Financial Chronicle,* November 30, 1901, Vol.
LXXIII, p. 1138; cf. also *Poor's Manual of Railroads,* 1883. As
to whether Harriman and the banking house of Kuhn, Loeb and
Co. had any connection with Standard Oil prior to the reorganization of the Union Pacific, I cannot say. Subsequent to the completion of that reorganization in 1897 there is no doubt that Harriman became the recognized representative of Standard Oil railroad
interests.

Union Pacific. As early as 1895 it had been formed to carry out some plan looking toward a rehabilitation of the financial standing of the road, but nothing was accomplished until the property was sold under foreclosure in 1897. It was then bought in by a reorganization committee which was in agreement with the syndicate headed by Kuhn, Loeb and Company.[38]

After the reorganization had been carried through by the latter, E. H. Harriman appeared as chairman of the executive committee, of which James Stillman was also a member. Representatives of the Gould interests, which had again gained control of the Union Pacific in 1890,[39] still held place on the board of directors, but they were evidently no longer of first importance. It was significant, however, that there should be found identified with a single property adherents of three different groups. Clearly indications were not lacking of the manner in which there was gradually to be brought about an advance toward an increasingly comprehensive form of combination, for the purpose of acquiring the gains made possible by a wide extension of investments.

---

[38]On agreement with the reorganization committee this syndicate provided $44,000,000 in cash, receiving in return for each $1,000 advanced, $1,000 par value 4 per cent. first-mortgage bonds and $500 par value preferred shares of the company.

[39]*Commercial and Financial Chronicle,* November 29, 1890, Vol. LI, p. 748; directors' lists in *Poor's Manual of Railroads.*

Along with the growth of the railroad interests a new movement began to develop about the beginning of 1898; for with the return of prosperity after a period of prolonged financial distress there was a marked launching out of the various groups of investors into the field of the "industrials." Some years before, adverse court decisions had led to the abrogation of all trust agreements which had for the most part been succeeded by holding companies made possible by the New Jersey law of 1889.[40] A few new companies had also been formed, such as the Diamond Match Company and the New York Biscuit Company (both Moore organizations), but as yet the holding company was not an important factor in the industrial field.

But with the inauguration of the era of the so-called "industrials" came notable combinations in the iron and steel trades. J. P. Morgan and Company and their allies, having acquired an assured position in the railroad world, now made their entry into the field of the industrials as organizers of Federal Steel (September, 1898).[41]

[40]The Standard Oil organization existed without taking advantage of the New Jersey law until 1899, a community of interests being maintained through the manner of distribution of the stocks of the various companies composing the "trust."

[41]The stocks of the companies it was proposed to combine having been secured (or, at any rate, a sufficient proportion of them) were then turned over to the new corporation together with

It was said that the profits of the firm derived from its services in organizing were about $200,-000,[42] but, apart from that consideration, the Morgan representation on the directorate of Federal Steel would indicate that a very substantial interest in the company had been acquired, although Standard Oil men were no doubt the dominant factor.[43]

The year following the formation of the Federal Steel Company, Morgan succeeded in uniting the leading tube works of the country into a single organization, the National Tube Company,[44] and in April, 1900, he assumed charge of

---

$14,075,000 in cash (such part as was not furnished by stock assessments being guaranteed by Morgan). In return, $53,000,000 preferred and $46,000,000 common stock of the Federal Steel Company was received by the organizers to be used in paying for the underlying properties.

[42]Report of the Industrial Commission, Vol. I, pp. 986 ff. (testimony of Judge Gary).

[43]In substantiation of this statement it may be mentioned that Standard Oil men had been connected with the Minnesota Iron Company (an important underlying property of Federal Steel) since 1887. Moreover, H. H. Rogers was a member of the executive committee of Federal Steel, and Roswell P. Flower, who had come to be closely identified with Standard Oil financiers through his copper interests, was a large holder of the company's stock. After his death, in May, 1899, it is probable that the Standard's hold on the property was materially strengthened. Cf. *Bradstreet's*, May 20, 1899, Vol. XXVII, p. 306; September 30, 1899, Vol. XXVII, p. 612.

[44]Standard Oil men were certainly associated with this enterprise, if the presence of Daniel O'Day, connected with the Standard Oil pipe-line system, and Jacob Vandergrift, one-time president of the United Pipe Lines Co., on the directorate of the company can be considered in the least significant.

the underwriting for another large steel "trust,"
the American Bridge Company.[45]   During
this same prolific period W. H. and J. H. Moore
sprang into prominence as organizers of the
American Tin Plate, National Steel (February,
1899), American Steel Hoop (April, 1899), and
American Sheet Steel (March, 1900) companies[46]—all four of which came to be controlled
by the small coterie of men for whom the Moores
had been acting.[47]   The only other important
steel combination prior to the formation of the

---

[45]Both in the case of the National Tube Company and in that
of the American Bridge Co., Morgan was given power to direct
their policy absolutely for a stated number of months; nine months
in the case of the former, and eighteen months in the case of the
latter.

[46]Judge Moore explained the manner in which these organizations were effected, as follows: "I will not charge you anything,"
he reports himself as having said to the owners of the companies
it was proposed to unite. "I will buy your properties and formu-
late a plan, and if you do not want to go into the new plan, you
can take cash." (Cf. testimony of W. H. Moore, Report of the
Industrial Commission, Vol. I, p. 963.)

[47]The nucleus of the Moore group consisted of certain iron
and steel manufacturers interested at one time in the various
companies that went to make up the four new combinations. The
group later extended its investments, branching out into the
domain of railroads.   It bought control of the Chicago, Rock
Island and Pacific (1901), reorganized it as the Rock Island
Company, and took over other properties, purchasing the St. Louis
and San Francisco (May, 1903.), and entering into an alliance
with the Seaboard Air Line the next October.   The financiers
composing the group are, however, relatively weak, and the
chances are that they are scarcely in a position to be considered
an independent power at the present time.   In all probability
their railroad management has come under the tutelage of
Standard Oil.

United States Steel Corporation was the American Steel and Wire Company (1899), at whose head stood John W. Gates.

As the panic of 1893 made for a growth both in the diversity and in the size of the fortunes of particular financiers, so the industrial depression, which set in toward the close of 1899 and continued through 1900, was occasion of profit to certain wealthy groups of investors who coerced certain other groups into alliance with them. At that time, conditions within the iron and steel trades were peculiarly severe, and with so many important groups of investors represented therein, a competitive struggle on a more comprehensive scale than ever before experienced might be fairly deduced. As a matter of fact, the formation of the United States Steel Company in 1901 seems to have been the outgrowth of some such struggle.

The evidence points strongly in the direction of a shrewdly planned attack by the joint Carnegie-Rockefeller forces against the other groups interested. In order to understand the situation, it is necessary to enter somewhat minutely into the relations formerly existing between the Carnegie and the Rockefeller interests in the Minnesota iron regions. The Oliver Iron Mining Company, a Carnegie property, which was one of the

largest shippers of ore on the Mesaba range, had
in 1896, made a fifty-year contract with the Lake
Superior Consolidated Iron Mines Company,
whereby, upon payment of a certain royalty, it
obtained possession of two rich mines on the Mesaba, guaranteeing in return a minimum annual
output of 600,000 tons of ore, to be shipped over
the Rockefeller road, the Duluth, Missabe, and
Northern, and carried in vessels belonging to the
Rockefeller fleet.[48] These shipments, together
with the output from the Oliver mines, ensured
an annual tonnage of from 1,200,000 to 1,500,000
tons.[49]

Although the Lake Superior Consolidated
Iron Mines Company continued to increase the
carrying capacity of its lake fleets for some years
subsequent to this contract, it was by no means
secure in its hold upon the transportation of the
Carnegie ore. By 1899 the Oliver Iron Mining
Company had by the acquirement of new holdings attained to an average annual output of
perhaps 4,000,000 or 4,500,000 tons of ore,[50] and,
obviously it would be advantageous to carry such
part of its own output as had not been disposed

[48]*Iron Age,* December 31, 1896, Vol. LVIII, pp. 1309, 1310;
James H. Bridge, The Inside History of the Carnegie Steel Company, Chap XVII, p. 259.

[49]*Iron Trade Review,* March 11, 1897, Vol. XXX.

[50]*Ibid.,* April 27, 1899, Vol. XXXII.

of by contract. Accordingly, the properties of the Lake Superior Iron Company were bought, and with them its fleet of six vessels, which were turned over to the newly formed Pittsburg Steamship Company (1899)[51]—by 1900 the third largest fleet on the lake.[52]

It now began to be rumored that not so long before this time, Mr. Rockefeller had offered to sell his large ore properties as well as his steamship and railway holdings to Mr. Carnegie for $50,000,000, and that it was the refusal of this offer which led to the adoption of coercive measures, taking shape in an attempt to corner the lake shipping in 1900.[53] However that may be, the Bessemer Steamship Company (the fleet of The Lake Superior Consolidated Iron Mines Company) purchased in the fall of 1899 the thirty vessels of the American Steel Barge Company, and these, together with the twenty-four or more already owned, gave it a dominant position in the lake ore shipping. The ore of the Oliver Iron Mining Company shipped under the contract of 1896 was taken at a rate which was an average of the wild and contract rates of each season. In an endeavor to keep up the wild

---

[51]*Iron Trade Review,* November 16, 1899, Vol. XXXII.
[52]*Iron Age,* May 10, 1900, p. 5, Vol. LXV.
[53]*Iron Age,* October 19, 1899, p. 300, Vol. LXIV.

rates so as to force this ore to pay a lake tonnage of $1.25, all but twenty of the vessels owned by the Bessemer Steamship Company were laid up.[54] As a result of this action the Carnegie Company made public its intention of building its own railroad from the Minnesota mines to the lake. Furthermore, it was announced (July, 1900) that the Carnegie Company proposed the erection of "what would probably be the largest rod-mill ever built."[55] The bearing of this proposal upon the situation becomes apparent if it be remembered that the plan to build a rod-mill would, if carried out, put a serious competitor in the field against the Federal Steel Company—a property in which Standard Oil interests were prominent. As matters stood, both sides bade fair to prove losers in the pending struggle, and there was little reason for surprise when it was announced in August that harmony had been once more decreed and new and satisfactory traffic agreements entered into.[56] The amicable working arrangements thus effected between the two interests continued from this time on until both were absorbed into the United

---

[54]*Iron Age,* June 14, 1900, p. 26 f., Vol. LXV.

[55]*Commercial and Financial Chronicle,* July 28, 1900, Vol. LXXI, p. 184.

[56]*Iron Age,* August 9, 1900, p. 4, Vol. LXVI.

States Steel Company. Whether the formation of the latter was hastened because of this union is a question open for debate. But certainly, apart from any active personal support which Mr. Carnegie may have received in his efforts to dispose of his holdings,[57] the increased control over the ore situation obtained by his alliance with the Rockefeller interests added to the strategic value of his position.

The campaign of aggression, initiated in 1900 with an attack upon the Federal Steel and the American Steel Hoop companies,[58] was continued without abatement from this time forth. The situation was peculiarly favorable, indeed, to the success of Mr. Carnegie's plans. In the earlier part of the year the iron and steel trades had suffered a relapse from a condition of overstimulated prosperity, and it needed only the closing of the mills of the American Steel and Wire Company "on account of an excessive accumulation of supplies"[59] to start a decline in the prices of steel stocks. By the end of June, 1900, quo-

[57] He was admittedly anxious to "sell out."

[58] The American Steel Hoop Co. was hit by the suggestion that the Carnegie Co. "might go into the manufacture of hoops and bands." Cf. *Commercial and Financial Chronicle*, July 28, 1900, Vol. LXXI, p. 1840.

[59] *Commercial and Financial Chronicle*, April 28, 1900, Vol. LXX, p. 843.

tations had been cut down more than half in the case of the common stocks, and preferred holdings had lost from 13 to 20 points. In November, when speculative securities were just beginning to be salable once more,[60] the Carnegie Company made further announcement of its intention to manufacture sheet steel, steel wire and nails, and steel pipes—an intention which, if carried out, was likely to produce a general demoralization in steel stocks. The Morgan interests were endangered as well as the Moore and Gates properties, and consternation was widespread. When, therefore, the Carnegie Company, early in January, 1901, announced the immediate construction of large tube-works at Conneaut,[61] Mr. Morgan, as the representative of the National Tube Company, as well as of other organizations that had been threatened, was compelled to enter into negotiations looking toward the purchase of the Carnegie holdings.[62] By the end of February, a consolidation of the leading steel companies of the country was announced, with J. P. Morgan and Company as organizers. It is no surprise to learn that the property of the Carnegie Company was taken over at an exceedingly liberal valua-

---

[60]Meade, *Trust Finance,* Chap. XI, pp. 213 ff.
[61]*Iron Trade Review,* January 10, 1901, Vol. XXXIV.
[62]*Iron Age,* February 7, 1901, p. 33, Vol. LXVII.

tion, Mr. Carnegie alone receiving approximately $217,720,000 in 5 per cent. first-mortgage gold bonds for his individual holdings.[63] As for the rest of the companies incorporated, the Lake Superior Consolidated Iron Mines obtained the most favorable terms,[64] although the majority secured bonuses both in preferred and in common stock.

Notwithstanding the resultant condition of inflation, it was thought that the Morgan syndicate had reaped an immense profit as the result of its operations.[65] But this belief was considerably shaken by the proposed bond-conversion scheme of the following year,[66] and subsequent events served to strengthen a gradually growing conviction that Morgan had not acted

---

[63]J. H. Bridge, *The Inside History of the Carnegie Steel Company,* Chap. XXIII, pp. 363, 364; also Moody, *The Truth About the Trusts,* p. 154.

[64]*Moody's Manual of Corporation Securities,* 1904, p. 1616.

[65]Some estimates put its gain as high as $56,500,000 (*Iron Age,* February 6, 1902; cf. also *Commercial and Financial Chronicle,* May 2, 1903, Vol. LXXVI, p. 977).

[66]The plan (ratified May, 1902,) contemplated the exchange at par of $2,000,000 of 7 per cent. cumulative preferred stock of the corporation for 5 per cent. second-mortgage gold bonds. As a result of litigation it did not go into effect until March, 1903. From May 16 to November 19 the syndicate enjoyed the sole right of conversion. It is estimated that it exchanged $104,300,000 of stock during a period in which, although bond quotations were falling, prices of preferred stock were falling relatively even lower. The conversion plan may have been merely a clever profit-making device or it may have been a desperate remedy adopted by men laden with securities of which they were unable to dis-

altogether as a voluntary agent. Perhaps he had
been "held up," so to speak, and forced to take
over properties at a valuation that later made it
difficult to dispose of the securities of the new
company to advantage.   Opinions upon this
point may vary, however, but that the organization of the United States Steel Company was
undertaken primarily for the purpose of securing harmony among the several groups interested
in the underlying companies is a conclusion fairly
deducible from a consideration of the incidents
leading up to the consolidation.

It is not possible even to indicate all the other
lines of corporate investment which these same
financiers were entering during the period from
1897 and 1898 onward. Some of the new holdings which were being acquired by the Standard
Oil group may be mentioned briefly, however.
As early as 1898 their interest in the Western
Union Telegraph Company began to develop,[67]

---

pose. At any rate, opposition to it led to a dissolution of the
syndicate earlier than had been expected (November, 1903,).
For an account of bond conversion and litigation, cf. Meade,
*The United States Steel Corporation Bond Conversion, Quar-
terly Journal of Economics*, Vol. XVIII, p. 22; also *Commercial
and Financial Chronicle*, November 21, 1903; *Moody's Manual
of Corporation Securities*, 1904, pp. 1613, 1634; Ripley, *The
Later History of the Steel Corporation Bond Conversion, Quar-
terly Journal of Economics*, Vol. XIX, p. 316.

[67]Roswell G. Rolston, president of the Farmers' Loan and
Trust Company, affiliated with Standard Oil, and likewise a "Na-

thus bringing them into contact with another important group of financiers, the Goulds.   In 1898 Standard Oil men launched the Amalgamated Copper Company, in which Morgan interests were likewise represented.[68]   The death of Roswell P. Flower (May, 1899), who was prominently identified with the copper trust, brought other property into the hands of Standard Oil men, since they bought largely of his stock holdings, notably securities of the Brooklyn Rapid Transit Company, of which it is said they subsequently gained control.[69]   The American Smelting and Refining Company (1899) was organized under Standard Oil influence,[70] and some years later (1903) entrance was secured into the Colorado Fuel and Iron Company, with which latter venture the Gould group was again associated.[71]   In the same year there was rumor of an alliance between the Standard Oil and the Wid-

---

tional City" man, became a director of the Western Union Telegraph Co. in 1897; James Stillman entered the board in 1898 or 1899; while Henry M. Flagler and Charles Lockhart, both "original" Standard Oil men, and E. H. Harriman went in in 1900.

[68]Frederick P. Olcott and Robert E. Bacon were among the directors.

[69]*Bradstreet's* May 20, 1899, Vol. XXVII, p. 306; September 30, 1899, Vol. XXVII, p. 612.

[70]*Commercial and Financial Chronicle,* April 15, 1899, Vol. LXVIII, p. 668.

[71]Concerning the Colorado Fuel and Iron Co., cf. *Bradstreet's,* November and December, 1902, June and December, 1903.

ener-Ryan parties with a view to the purchase of
the Metropolitan Securities Company. All idea
of such purchase was vigorously denied at the
time, but as Ryan subsequently took possession
of the property, the denial lost somewhat of its
force.[72]

While Standard Oil was thus engaged in acquiring holdings in the corporations mentioned,
as well as in others that might be named, the
group was at the same time extending its great
railway system by purchase and by alliance. In
1899 a syndicate composed of Gould, Schiff,
Harriman, and Stillman, had purchased a controlling interest in the Chicago and Alton.[73] In
1900 Harriman, Stillman, and Gould combined
to buy out the Kansas City Southern[74]—a road
which had been a disturbing factor in the western rate situation.

---

[72]*Commercial and Financial Chronicle,* September 5, 1903, Vol.
LXXVII, p. 511.

[73]John D. Rockefeller's name was first mentioned in place of
Stillman's as a member of the syndicate (cf. *Commercial and
Financial Chronicle,* February 11, 1899, and *Bradstreet's,* Feb-
ruary 25, 1899,). An investigation of the Interstate Commerce
Commission (New York City, January 6, 1907,) brought out the
fact that the Chicago and Alton was under the joint control of
the Chicago, Rock Island, and Pacific Railway and the Union
Pacific, one road having charge of it one year; the other, the next.
The arrangement grew out of a contract between Harriman and
Leeds, entered into in 1904.

[74]*Bradstreet's,* November 3, 1900, Vol. XXVIII, p. 692.

The facts just mentioned are important in that they bear witness to a growing community of interests between the Standard Oil and the Gould adherents. But the events of the next few months were to be of even greater significance. In 1901 the Harriman-Kuhn-Loeb syndicate, on behalf of the Union Pacific, which was dominated by Standard Oil, acquired control of the Huntington-Speyer interests in the Southern Pacific for $40,000,000 or $50,000,000[75]—a purchase which added greatly to the power of the group in the western railroad world. The same year was marked by the entrance of Standard Oil into the Northern Pacific under the leadership of Harriman.[76] The raid which resulted in their gaining control of the stock[77] and securing, as they thought, a "say-so" as to the disposal of the Chi-

---

[75]*Bradstreet's*, February 9, 1901, Vol. XXIX, p. 84.

[76]It is probable that Standard Oil men had an interest in the Northern Pacific prior to this time. They were creditors of the road when it went into bankruptcy in 1893; F. T. Gates, a representative of John D. Rockefeller, and James Stillman were members of a committee to arrange for a collateral trust agreement to extinguish the floating debt. (Cf. Commercial and Financial Chronicle, May 20, 1893.) Subsequent to the reorganization, John D. Rockefeller and James Stillman were mentioned as members of the new board (ibid., Oct. 17, 1896). Rockefeller's name did not appear thereafter, however, but Stillman continued as director, and in 1897 Oliver H. Payne also became a member of the board.

[77]*Commercial and Financial Chronicle*, May 11, 1901, Vol. LXXII, p. 936; October 12, 1901, Vol. LXXIII, p. 783; October 19, 1901, Vol. LXXIII, p. 843.

cago, Burlington and Quincy, the joint purchase
of the Great Northern and the Northern Pacific,
was a short-lived victory. Morgan and his allies
still held a majority of the common stock, which
carried with it a provision to retire the preferred
holdings at any time at par. This they threatened to do, and the result was a compromise—
the formation of the Northern Securities Company, November, 1901, in which all three interests involved—Standard Oil, Morgan, and Hill
—were represented.

It was in 1901, too, that George Gould acquired control of the Denver and Rio Grande
and the Rio Grande and Western.[78] The next
year he purchased the West Virginia Central
and the Western Maryland,[79] while shortly thereafter it was noised abroad that Standard Oil had
acquired large holdings in a Gould road, the
Missouri Pacific,[80] and that the two interests
were working in harmony.[81]

---

[78]*Railway Age,* May 17, 1901, Vol. XXXI, p. 531.

[79]*Bradstreet's,* July 12, 1902, Vol. XXX, p. 436.

[80]*Ibid.,* September 13, 1902, p. 578. The appearance on the
directorate of the Missouri Pacific of E. P. Prentice, John D.
Rockefeller's son-in-law, F. T. Gates, and John D. Rockefeller,
Jr., would tend to verify reports as to stock purchases. Cf.
Poor's Manual of Railroads.

[81]*Bradstreet's,* September 13, 1902, Vol. XXX, p. 578. A
statement was likewise made with reference to another road as
follows: "St. Paul, as is well known, is dominated by Standard
Oil."

As early as 1900 it had been rumored that Standard Oil men had entered the territory of the New York Central, the Vanderbilt stronghold. During 1904 their interests were markedly increased, while the relations between the Union Pacific and the New York Central came to be regarded as especially close. Furthermore, Standard Oil and Vanderbilt representatives were operating in joint control of the Delaware, Lackawanna, and Western,[82] and it may fairly be said that all the available evidence would indicate that there was a very substantial identity of interests between the groups in question.

In February, 1905, the Union Pacific secured a representation in the Atchison, Topeka and Santa Fe[83]—practically annexed it, in fact, and thus added materially to the mileage of the so-called Harriman system of railroads. There is no doubt that Standard Oil was back of a notable and very recent victory won by Mr. Harriman, who led the fight against the president of the Illinois Central, whom he succeeded in deposing, thereby demonstrating the power which he and

---

[82] Cf. *Commercial and Financial Chronicle*, February 24, 1894, Vol. LVIII, p. 345; cf. also *Moody's Manual of Corporation Securities*, 1904, for list of directors.

[83] In the persons of H. H. Rogers and H. C. Frick. It has been recently divulged that the Oregon Short Line bought $10,-000,000 of the preferred stock of the Santa Fe, subsequent to July 1, 1906.

his backers could exert in controlling the policy of the road.[84]

The conclusion that must be reached in any case after even a superficial review of the facts, is that the financial interests in control of the great railroad systems of the country have become connected in one way or another in almost inextricable fashion. Furthermore, it looks as if the Harriman (Standard Oil) and the Morgan groups are coming to hold first place among these various interests, and indications are not lacking to support the belief that the Standard Oil group may one day come to occupy the position of chief control. At any rate, its aggressive policy has thus far been exceedingly successful, and the wealth and power of its chief members have grown with surprising rapidity. To mention the most notable of their achievements, they have, within the space of a few years, acquired control of the Huntington properties, allied themselves to some extent with the Goulds,[85] secured a portion of the Vanderbilt holdings, en-

---

[84]In a hearing before the Interstate Commerce Commission (New York, January, 1907,) it was learned that the Oregon Short Line, part of the Harriman system, owned securities of the Illinois Central to the amount of $28,123,100, which had been acquired since July 1, 1906. The same road held $39,540,600 of the stock of the Baltimore and Ohio, also acquired since July, 1906.

croached upon the Morgan-Hill territory, and made their way into other roads less closely identified with particular groups.

Moreover, it may be well to state that, as the Standard Oil group extended its investment activities and came into closer contact with other groups, the National City Bank began to contract new alliances, to admit representatives of outside interests to its directorate, and to purchase control of other banks, until today it stands at the head of one of the most powerful financial organizations in the country. Nor has the growth of this aggregation ceased, for each year the National City banks are becoming more closely allied with that other important chain of institutions, the so-called Morgan banks. The practically endless series of interrelations that have thus been brought about points strongly in the direction of a complete unification of control of these financial institutions, to be concentrated in the hands of that group of financiers, who shall eventually come to dominate the general investment field. As approach is made toward this final stage of development, it becomes more and more difficult

---

[85]Since George J. Gould decided to build the Western Pacific, his relations with Harriman are apparently not so close as formerly. Cf. hearing, January, 1907, Interstate Commerce Commission, New York City.

adequately to estimate the fortune of any single member of a group. The amount of his holdings is conditioned by the power of the group, and that power expresses itself through group action, the acquisitive potentialities of such action being impossible of measurement.

CHAPTER V.

PERSONAL AND NON-PERSONAL FACTORS INVOLVED IN GAIN GETTING.

E VEN superficial studies of the business career of John Jacob Astor emphasize its supposedly dualistic nature and distinguish between the apparently sharply defined aspects of gain getting for which it stands. In fact, Astor's trading operations are frequently discussed as if they had not the slightest theoretical connection with his activities as an investor in land. It is the latter method of fortune getting which is generally considered to afford exclusive opportunity for the appearance of an "unearned increment," that is, gain of some sort which cannot be attributed to the personal effort or personal ability of the beneficiary. Under the influence of this misconception, an attempt is made to distinguish between the profits arising from trade, and the gains growing out of land investments, on the ground that, in the one case, the size of the returns is conditioned by the degree of personal activity, whereas, in the other case, no appreciable amount of individual effort or ability is involved.

Daniel Webster, for instance, in an address to the jury, when arguing against Astor's claim to lands in Putnam county, implied some such distinction between commercial exertions and land investments, in connection with the moral judgment that he passed upon Astor. True, his argument was impassioned and polemical in tone. Moreover, he was referring to a particular case of land investment, characterized by certain peculiar features. But the antithesis that he suggests is nevertheless significant—the more so that it was designed to appeal to popular prejudices. His plea was that Astor had obtained possession of the land in dispute, "not as he did that vast wealth than which no one envies him less than I do—not by fair and honest exertions in commercial enterprise, but by speculation, by purchasing up the forlorn hope of the heirs of a family driven from the country by a bill of attainder."[1] Whether designedly or not, Webster has here made a distinction between "commercial exertions" and "speculation" in land, implying, in the one case, that the source of returns is personal activity, in the other, that the gains are to be attributed in the main to a non-personal factor—that is, to some cause operative to produce gain, irrespective of individual effort or of individual ability.

---

[1]Jackson vs. Carver, U. S. Circuit Court, Southern District of New York.

It is on the basis of this broad division into personal and non-personal factors conditioning gain, that an analysis will be made, not only of the returns that came to Astor from trade and from land investments, but likewise of the incomes from various sources enjoyed by Gould, and by members of the "Standard Oil" and "Morgan" groups of investors. Further, it will be shown that, given such a principle of differentiation, no rigid line of demarcation can be drawn between these various methods of gain getting. This proposition once established, the classification will receive a more extensive application, with intent to determine the nature of the gains that arise in the course of the general process of fortune accumulation. Finally, the significance of the analysis for purposes of present-day criticism will be discussed.[2]

The Astor fortune alone furnishes strong evidence to support the assertion that no one method of gain getting represents the exclusive operation either of personal or of non-personal factors. Even in the case of Astor's most active trading

[2]The method of treatment proposed leaves strictly on one side all question concerning the social services rendered by owners of large fortunes, since that is a problem properly and logically separate from the present task. In fact, it is a subject the nature of whose treatment depends largely upon the sort of theoretical analysis which has preceded it. It will, therefore, be reserved for later discussion in this paper.

ventures, did there not arise an "unearned"[3] increment, plainly attributable to certain non-personal factors? The profits arising from his traffic with the Indians were due in large part to the superlative ignorance of that non-commercial people. Or, if this statement be objected to, as reflecting somewhat invidiously upon Astor, it must at any rate be conceded that such profits were the result of radically different standards of value. The schedules of exchange relating to the trade make ludicrous the assumption of a "freely competitive" state in which reward is considered to be in proportion to individual effort or ability. It is true that in the prosecution of the Indian trade a high degree of personal skill and of mental dexterity was requisite. This fact helped unduly to emphasize the importance of the individual. His pecuniary success was popularly supposed to have its source in personal activity alone. Consequently, the attendant non-personal factors were relegated to a position of obscurity, although, as has been shown, a closer examination reveals their overwhelming importance.[4]

---

[3]The term "unearned" is retained simply to show the variety of phenomena to which it may be applied if its use be logically extended. It is taken to connote absence of personal activity.

[4]Other illustrations might be drawn from the China trade. The peculiar tastes of the Chinese were a source of exceptional gain to the Yankee shipper, especially when the latter could obtain the commodities desired by the former at relatively low prices, as in the case of furs.

On the other hand, land investments frequently afford striking examples of value accretion, associated with only a minimum of personal activity. Hence they are thought of almost exclusively when the subject of the "unearned increment" is discussed. Yet, even in such cases there must have been some sort of initial activity put forth by the owner of the land. For example, Astor needed to exercise unusual discrimination in order to decide in what direction the city of New York was likely to grow, and to estimate the possibilities of that development. Granted that, it will be asked, could any appreciable proportion of the $18,000,000 worth of real estate owned by him at the time of his death, be held to represent a return due to his personal efficiency? Given the existing system of business relations, the whole amount of the property was legally and legitimately due him. But can it, in logic, be said that an explanation should assign a fixed percentage of the accumulation to the category of returns due to efficiency? The fact that Astor was possessed of greater business astuteness than the average man helped to explain why he, rather than someone else, came into possession of this landed property. Superior personal ability is in general exceedingly potent in aiding the individual to acquire property as against other

individuals. But personal ability does not for
that reason adequately explain the "how much"
of those acquisitions.[5] A determination of questions of ownership is not a determination of questions concerning the amount of gain arising as
the result of ownership.

Too often, the importance of the existing system of social institutions and legal relations, as
conditioning the process of gain getting, is un-
derrated. Distributive questions are apt to be
discussed in a manner to indicate that the distributive process takes place in some sublimated
sphere that knows no law but a "natural" law.
The emphasis is thrown on questions of skill, of
productive efficiency. The formally efficient conditioning factors are not felt to disturb to any
great extent these more "vital" causes making
for gain. But it cannot be repeated too often
that the institution of private property presupposes a whole system of formal legal arrangements, within which the individual must operate
in the process of gain getting. The exceptionally or even ordinarily clever man may succeed as
against his fellows in acquiring title to a certain
amount of property. Very possibly (although

---

[5]Given a start, the influence of acquired wealth upon further
accumulation has also a bearing upon the present discussion.
This point will be taken up later.

not invariably) he is enabled to do this as a result of industry and a disposition to save, combined with a certain keenness of judgment in making investments. But does it follow that the amount of property owned by such a man measures the degree of ability possessed by him, as compared with some other man? By no means. Property is an acquisitive category; it is a case of mine against thine, and, conceivably, ever so slight a difference in personal equipment may give one man ownership of a piece of property as against a rival.

But, admitting an exceptional degree of personal ability, suppose that an individual gets possession of a property sure to bring in large returns in the future without further effort on his part. Are those future returns all to be accredited to the more or less of superior ability that enabled him to acquire possession of the property in the first place? To take the most obvious illustration, assume that he has purchased an acre of land for $100; twenty years later the city has surrounded this lot, and he sells it for $100,000. In this case, it has been taken for granted that the owner had the foresight to predicate some such result (although it may very well have been an accident), and that this foresight was the efficient cause of the original purchase. Even so, do the gains derivable from such a purchase in any way measure the personal ability of the owner? He might, perhaps, have sold his land for $50,000 or for $200,000, and it would not have been possible to say that he had displayed greater or less acumen in making his original purchase. Social changes, partly predicable, but for the most part incalculable, have brought about the increased gain. The factor of personal ability has, in such cases, merely determined who is to be the recipient of those gains under the existing laws of property.

Hence, it is easy to see why, in the case of a landed fortune such as that of John Jacob Astor, the overweening part played by social factors in increasing the value of Astor's land holdings, frequently caused the element of personal ability conditioning the returns derived from such investments to be wholly ignored. To the uncritical mind, such a form of gain appeared to be entirely the result of social conditions and legal arrangements. It therefore acquired the highly derogatory appellation "unearned," because of the persistence of the idea that reward "generally" is, and hence always should be, in proportion to personal effort or personal ability.

Jay Gould, as well as John Jacob Astor, won a large part of his fortune as the result of purely speculative operations. Indeed, no great fortune either before or since his day seems to have been more consistently derived from what, in the larger sense of the term, was gambling—a game, too, in which Gould, generally speaking, held the bag. Hence, it is easy to show that the resultant gains were in many instances almost wholly the result of the peculiar circumstances conditioning his activity, and were in that sense and to that extent "unearned."

No one questions that Gould had a peculiarly sinister type of ability, that he was an excessively shrewd as well as a calmly resolute man. His cleverness enabled him to manipulate situations, so as to derive from them the utmost individual profit. But, even when these returns were legally acquired, did they afford even an approximate measure of his personal ability, of the accuracy of his judgment? By no manner of means. He was generally in a position where he took no chances; he stood to win in the very nature of things. His stock speculations in the Erie, for instance, were certainly not due to any foresight on his part, as to whether the stock was likely to rise or to fall. It generally rose or fell as he dictated; and he was enabled to dictate its price fluctuations, and to profit thereby, because of the unlimited power he exercised over

the policy of the Erie, by reason of the fiduciary
position he occupied.

Further, the conditions prevailing throughout
the country during the period immediately succeeding the Civil War were eminently favorable
to advancing the fortunes of any cool-headed
speculator in stocks, even when he did not have
the treasury of a great railroad at his disposal.
A demoralized, speculative fever had taken possession of the country; the large issues of paper
money, giving rise to the premium on gold, the
excessive expenditures of the government made
necessary by the war—all had contributed to ag-
gravate the situation. There were lambs to fleece
in plenty, who were just as ignorant of the possibilities of the speculative market as were the
Indians of the fur-trader's wiles. The advantage
enjoyed by a speculator who had "inside information," because he occupied a (so-called) position
of trust within the councils of a corporation,
made a contest with him as unequal as any trade
between Indian and white man.

But it was not only as a speculator that Gould
enjoyed gains largely conditioned by non-personal factors. As an investor in great public service corporations—notably the Manhattan Elevated Railway Company and the Western Union
Telegraph Company—he profited in proportion

as these companies profited by the growth in wealth and power of the communities which they served.

To take another illustration, it would be impossible to deny the great ability as worker and organizer displayed by John D. Rockefeller, while actively connected with the refining business. Is it, therefore, possible to say that the many millions which he derived from his connection with the Standard Oil Company furnish a measure of that ability? Granting that a certain sort of ability is the *sine qua non* of pecuniary success, that ability is not alone adequate to explain the degree of success. There are all sorts of non-personal factors to be considered, as, for instance, in the case of the Standard Oil Company, the gains resulting from the favors extended by the railroads during an era of fierce competitive strife. The attitude of the railroads aided greatly in building up the monopoly power of the company with all its attendant advantages. Further, with the increase in size of this great industrial concern, it came to approximate more closely to the position of a public service corporation, such as a railway or a telegraph company, and to profit more largely, therefore, from the growth in wealth and power of the country at large.

The testimony which has been offered is, no doubt, sufficiently varied to establish the fact of the joint operation under all conditions of both personal and non-personal factors. This proposition once established, it can therefore be stated as a corollary not requiring demonstration that, between those methods of gain getting in which the personal element looms large, and those in which it has become a negligible factor, there must exist all conceivable varieties of combination of the two factors. Hence, there must everywhere be found "unearned increments," differing widely in amount, with variations in the relative importance of the attendant non-personal factors.

The discussion, as thus far given, has not been directly concerned with the manner of growth of these great fortunes; the treatment has, in fact, been analytical rather than developmental. It is, however, a matter of much importance to determine whether the gains, which make possible further accumulations, are largely conditioned by personal ability, or whether non-personal considerations attain constantly increasing prominence in aiding the process of growth. Could it be shown that the general tendency is in the latter direction, some light would be thrown upon the causes of the rancor manifested against men of great fortune—a rancor that, given the strongly individualistic commercial preconceptions of the community, is otherwise hardly capable of a logical explanation. But, before arriving at any decision upon this point, it will be necessary to discuss the nature of those factors which become increasingly operative with the increase in size of a fortune.

In the case of very large fortunes, a continuance of growth sometimes seems so inevitable as almost to partake of the nature of a mechanical process. Of course, there is necessarily implied some sort of action on the part of the owners of such fortunes. This may, however, take the negative form of simply refraining from consuming the whole of the returns to which they are entitled, and it may entail little or none of the so-called abstinence supposed always to attach to the investment process. In fact, the incomes of exceptionally wealthy men are frequently so large that there remains a surplus, even after fancied needs of expenditure have been satisfied. Moreover, many American millionaires, such as Astor, Gould, and Rockefeller, who began life in poverty, are men of relatively simple tastes, who have no desire to expend more than a small proportion of the incomes due them. Consequently there ensues a bewildering process of in-

11

vestment and reinvestment,[6] which, assuming a continuance of ordinary conditions, gives rise to the phenomenon of unending growth.[7]

In later years, the corporate system has added greatly to the ease with which investment interests have been extended. By enabling an individual to exercise a power much in excess of that which he could wield if forced to make outright purchases in order to secure control of a company, it has opened up to him many more avenues of gain. No operations so extensive as those of present-day groups of investors would have been possible under a non-corporate system in which "abstract" rights of property in the form of stocks and bonds were unknown.[8] Moreover,

[6]The part played by the individual in determining the direction to be taken by these investments is considered in another connection.

[7]In discussing any great fortune, it should be remembered that pride in its mere size is an energizing principle of considerable force in the direction of activities looking toward further accumulations. The fortune comes to be regarded as an institutional fact, which should not suffer change, because of births, deaths, marriages, or other extraneous happenings. In consequence, there exists a disposition to transmit it intact to that descendant who gives best evidence of ability to conserve and to augment it. The heads of the Astor, Vanderbilt, and Gould families, all owning numerous descendants, have seen fit to select one or two of each generation as the guardians of the family fortunes, which they in their turn will be expected to transmit practically intact and greatly augmented to succeeding generations.

[8]For a discussion of the importance of "abstract property" in the making of large fortunes cf. G. P. Watkins, *The Growth of Large Fortunes*. Publication of the American Economic Association, November, 1907.

for speculative operations such as those of Jay Gould and many of the later men belonging to the Standard Oil and Morgan groups, the existence of "abstract property" is of primary importance. For Morgan, of course, as dealer in securities, and reorganizer of stock and bond-issuing companies, this "abstract property" is indispensable.

But for the gains derived during the process of growth of a great fortune from a simple extension of investment interests, the corporate system with its attendant feature of abstract, paper (?) property is not absolutely essential, however greatly it may facilitate the ease with which investments can be extended. Undoubtedly, the existence of rights of ownership in the form of negotiable securities (becoming daily larger in volume, as the corporate system extends into new fields of industry) is of great and growing importance for the development of present-day fortunes—especially in so far as those fortunes come to be derived more and more from immense public-service corporations. But "abstract property" cannot be invoked as the sole explanation of the gains coming to men of great wealth. It is, after all, but one of the conditions growing out of social-legal arrangements, which aid the process of accumulation. Indeed, it should be re-

membered that the fortune of John Jacob Astor
was acquired long before the days of the Stock
Exchange, although it is not to be denied that his
real estate holdings offer a close analogy to the
stock and bond holdings of these latter days.[9]

It has been shown that the non-personal factor
of mere size largely conditions the ease with
which an individual may extend his investments
and thus augment his fortune. It also enables
him to take advantage of innumerable opportunities to invest under peculiarly favorable circumstances, and thereby to make still further
additions to the sum of his "unearned increments." One of the facts that stand out most
prominently to a person who is making a developmental study of large fortunes is the increase
in the amount and extent of investments, which
takes place just at those times when the community at large is suffering from acute financial
depression. Thus, during the War of 1812 and
the panic of 1837, Astor increased his holdings of
real estate enormously, as the result of numerous
mortgage foreclosures. Similarly, the panic of
1893 gave Morgan unrivalled opportunities to
obtain interests in numerous bankrupt roads, as
the price of undertaking their reorganization.

---

[9]Cf. G. P. Watkins, *The Growth of Large Fortunes,* pp. 43, 88.

Needless to say, the circumstances of the time enabled him to dictate the terms of settlement in a manner highly advantageous to himself. It is from this period of financial demoralization that Morgan and his adherents date their origin as a powerful group of investors. About the same time, "Standard Oil" men[10] were enabled to secure many valuable properties at low prices, notably the rich mines in the Lake Superior iron ore regions obtained by Mr. Rockefeller.

But apart from any widespread social disorder, there are numerous opportunities afforded a wealthy man to profit by individual cases of financial embarrassment or of superimposed necessity. Witness the case of Astor, who purchased the posts of the Northwest Company, after a law had been passed which made it illegal for the British organization to carry on business in this country. His purchase of the rights of the heirs to the Morris estate is likewise an illustration in point. Gould, for his part, profited upon many occasions through buying control of bankrupt companies at absurdly low prices, and then forcing other corporations to purchase them by means of threats. For example, he terrorized

---

10 A group of investors can of course force sales even more effectively than the single rich man, and they can take even prompter advantage of ill times.

the Union Pacific management into taking over
the Kansas Pacific and the Denver Pacific at inflated valuations, and he so injured the business
of the Western Union Telegraph Company that
it was compelled to come to terms with the Atlantic and Pacific, and with the American Union
telegraph companies, to the great gain of the two
last-named concerns. The advantage which Carnegie (backed, probably, by Rockefeller,) took of
the demoralization existing within the steel trade
in 1899-1900, to force a purchase of his interests,
adds another to the long list of possible illustrations. As a matter of fact, anyone can recall occasions upon which he has heard lesser business
men lamenting their inability to take advantage
of the exceptional opportunities for investment
afforded by "hard times" or by ill luck. But, as
it happens, they are opportunities enjoyed for the
most part by the man whose income greatly ex-
ceeds his current expenditures, and who is eager-
ly seeking new avenues of investment. He it is
who is the chief recipient of the benefits accruing
to a purchaser in cases of forced sale.

The particular direction taken by successive investments during the period of fortune accumulation is likewise a matter of much importance.
A judicious extension of investment interests
may result in the creation or strengthening of cer-

tain monopolistic (non-personal) factors, which will prove a source of exceptional gain to the individual. If Astor had carried on the fur trade as did so many others, without attempting to develop transportation and shipping facilities, the North American Fur Company could never have attained the strongly monopolistic position that it occupied in the middle west.[11] As it was, the monopoly once established, the chances of loss were reduced to a minimum, and full advantage could be taken of the favorable conditions inherent in the trade.

So in the case of the Standard Oil Company, its monopolistic powers were strengthened, and big gains were derived from the development of the pipe-line system, in connection with the refining business. Indeed, as investment interests in general become more and more ramified, there ensues a diminution of the chances of individual loss, consequently, a greater possibility that non-personal factors will operate to individual advantage. Hence the logic of that most highly developed type of financiering, which combines

---

[11]It is not meant to minimize the ability displayed by Astor in recognizing the advantages to be derived from developing facilities for transport. But the question at this point is, given that development, what other factors entered to condition the size of the returns. The matter of personal ability will be later discussed.

interests so varied in character, that it sometimes seems as if it embraced the entire field of trade and transportation. The greater the extent of such heterogeneous investments, the less likely it is that monopoly gains within one field will be curtailed by conditions operative within other lines of activity. The whole range of interests can, in short, be managed as a unit to give the largest possible individual returns.

As for the possibilities of speculative gain that arise with such an extension of holdings as has been effected during the last few years, they are incalculable. If Gould could send the stocks of the Erie and of several other roads up or down, as his purpose required, by reason of the control he exercised within a relatively limited field, what may not the "Standard Oil" or the "Morgan" group accomplish? They can send gas, electric, steel, street railway, and numerous other stocks up or down, as the case may be. A simple pronouncement of policy may be all that is necessary to bring about a startling change in stock quotations. The resultant gains can hardly be attributed, therefore, to the foresight and skill in taking risks of the men who bring about these fluctuations. It is the absence of risk due to the sheer extent of their interests which enables them to profit, with the exercise of a minimum amount of prudence. To quote Henry Clews, when speaking of one of these groups of financiers: "Their resources are so vast that they need only to concentrate on any given property in order to do with it what they please. . . . There is an utter absence of chance that is terrible to contemplate. This combination controls Wall Street almost absolutely. With such power and facility, it is easily conceivable that these men must make enormous gains on either side of the market."[12]

With the growth in size of a fortune, there generally occurs a change in the character of the personal activity of its owner. In fact, there is evidence of a continuous development of functional specialization on the part of the individual, which could not profitably have taken place at an earlier period. The fortune of John Jacob Astor serves to illustrate the process very distinctly. Astor was first seen wearily tramping the country in search of furs, trading with the Indians, negotiating with the merchants—in short, engaged in a business which involved a high degree of genuinely exhausting labor. Moreover, every detail of the existing crude organization required his personal attention, while he had also to look

---

[12]Quoted by Fetter in his *Principles of Economics,* p. 378.

sharply to the financial matters of income and
outgo. Eventually, the purely physical labors
connected with the trade devolved upon subordinates. Astor assumed the position of head manager. He directed the men in the field, decided
what territory should be covered, what goods
should be furnished, and what prices should be
offered. Not only did he thus order the general
policy of his undertakings, but he financed them
as well. Later, he transferred the more immediate control of the trade to trusted heads of de-
partments, reserving to himself a certain large
supervision, with a view to determining the nature and extent of his expenditures. Even Jay
Gould can show a similar advance from the hard-
ships endured as clerk in a small store, as surveyor, and as civil engineer, to the physically less
arduous position of manager of a tanning business. Then came his graduation into the speculative field. Henceforth, his activities were no
longer directed to details of management. He
was concerned with them only in so far as they affected the financial operations with which his time
was fully occupied. The same stages of development were passed through by John D. Rockefeller, and by any number of the wealthy financiers of the present day, saving always those who
started life already possessed of wealth.

Indeed, it is inevitable that there should take place these changes in the forms of personal activity of men of great wealth. Even the most energetic person, possessed of twenty-five, fifty, or a hundred millions of dollars, finds his time fully employed in looking after the financial details of management, in deciding when to invest in a new enterprise, when to withdraw from an old one, when to authorize fresh expenditures, when to retrench upon previous ones. Apart from the general supervision which such pecuniary interests entail, there is likely to be no opportunity afforded him for any immediate tasks of management and control—such tasks, for instance, as require expert technical knowledge, or ability to organize separate productive processes, or facility in effecting purchases and sales of materials. There is, of course, even less reason to expect that any sort of manual labor or physical effort will be put forth by the man of great wealth, although, if he be a self-made millionaire, he may have labored arduously, while his fortune was in the making.

From what has been said, it becomes evident that it would be quite useless to affirm or to deny that the personal element which figures in the process of fortune accumulation, becomes absolutely either greater or less with the growth in size of the fortune. As a matter of fact, the forms of activity are different in kind, hence, non-commensurable as regards degree. Taking the personal element for granted, therefore, all that can be ventured is the assertion that the non-personal factors conditioning the process of fortune accumulation attain an ever-increasing influence in affecting the size of the individual's gain.

It is an imperfect recognition of this fact, which is translated into the unreflective criticism that the rich man cannot have "earned" the fortune he has acquired. The implication is that he cannot possibly display an amount of individual activity or of personal ability as much greater as his reward is larger than that of other men. From what source, then, it is asked, can he have derived such unusual returns? It is not seen that they are due to all sorts of non-personal considerations, which must always be reckoned with, but which happen to have operated with peculiar force under the given conditions. Hence there is a disposition to attribute all such exceptional returns to undesirable institutions or to questionable practices of some sort.

Even production on a large scale is frequently condemned as a thing evil in itself and not to be tolerated, simply because it usually presupposes a considerable degree of monopolistic (non-personal) gain. Further, large-scale production is sometimes viewed with disfavor because, in so far as it has taken on a corporate form, it has facilitated an extension of investment interests through stock and bond purchases, and a consequent control of the market situation, which enables certain men to obtain speculative profits almost without risk of loss, and, it may be, with a minimum of effort. But to condemn large scale production itself, solely for such reasons, is to confuse the purely productive facts of industry with problems connected with the social aspects of distribution. There is, at any rate, no similar confusion in the minds of those who question the right to the "unearned increment" arising from private ownership of land. They, at least, propose to effect distributive changes (namely, the abolition of private property in land), as a remedy for what they regard as distributive evils, since they cannot, of course, inveigh against the existence of the land itself.

The same failure to appreciate the actual facts of fortune-building, the same desire to find "abnormal" causes of growth has led to bitter personal abuse of men of large fortune. Why? Their business morality is just as high, and frequently, no doubt, a little higher than that of the ordinary small town trader or money lender

(which is not saying that it in any way conforms
to the standard which an extra-commercial and
aroused public opinion would force upon them).
Why, it may be asked, have the petty shifts, the
ruthless bargaining, the unrelenting rivalries of
small producers and tradesmen been portrayed
without the slightest personal animus having been
manifested by the portrayer? Are the resultant
gains any less abnormal than the supposed or actual pilferings of the rich? Yet the parallelism
is rarely insisted upon. Why? Because to the
public at large, the gains of the lesser business
men do not seem so out of proportion to their
individual activity as to require explanation on
the ground of illegitimacy. Consequently, there
is seldom any attempt to scrutinize their methods very closely, although their gains are as sure-
ly leavened at times by fraud and sharp practice,
as are those of the wealthiest men in the land.
But when it comes to a consideration of the great
fortunes, there is a sudden change of attitude.
When it is seen that men such as Astor, Gould,
Rockefeller, Morgan, and others, may, by judicious purchase and sale of certain rights of ownership, add millions to the value of their properties, criticism at once becomes rife. However
great the ability displayed in effecting such transactions, it is felt to have no connection with the

size of the return, and the cry of "unearned" is at once raised. Then an explanation of the unusual gains of these men is sought for in their acts, rather than in the institutions and the situations which condition their activity. Their entire careers are gone over with an eye to searching out iniquity. If it be discovered (and it usually can be,[13] since few business transactions survive the test of non-commercial standards of conduct) it is then hastily inferred that dishonesty affords in large part an explanation for excessive wealth accumulations. In point of fact, the sharp practices of the average business man are just as dishonest and probably as widespread. Hence any sweeping condemnation of the man of great fortune on such ground involves both large and small. The result is an unconscious indictment of our whole system of business relations. Whether justly or not is irrelevant to the present inquiry.

---

[13]Notably in the case of Gould.

CHAPTER VI.

THE SOCIAL SERVICE RENDERED
BY OWNERS OF GREAT
FORTUNES.

A DISCUSSION of the personal and non-
personal factors involved in the acquiring
of large fortunes leaves on one side all speculation concerning the possible social services that
may be rendered while those fortunes are being
accumulated. That there exists a concept of social service is indubitable, but it is questionable
whether its content is the same for any two members of the same social group. For instance, a
big industrial or trading corporation ministers
to certain professed needs of large groups of
people. A system of railroads stands as tangible
evidence of service being rendered the community. But is there any way of measuring the positive social value of those services? For that matter, do people agree as to their exact nature? Is
it not necessary, moreover, to take into account
the social costs incurred as the price of obtaining
the positive services? Again, could more than a
rude and uncertain approximation be had?

How, for instance, judge of the degree of social service rendered by the North American Fur

Company? Some persons would extol the benefits arising from the introduction into the world markets of the skins so highly desired by civilized communities. Others would merely see the demoralizing effects of the trade upon the Indians, and the unnecessarily rapid destruction of the fur-bearing animals of the continent. To take another illustration, even the worst managed railways, such, for example, as the Erie under the direction of Gould, serve the communities through which they run. But who can estimate the disorders and injuries which may at the same time result from improper or dishonest conduct of the affairs of such roads? Simply to suggest a third problem, how equate the services and disservices to society resulting from the existence of the Standard Oil Company? Does not the decision as to whether or not a "positive good" has resulted depend in such cases more upon the temperament of the judge than upon the evidence?

The most that can be expected is a fairly general judgment that in specific cases the advantages derived by society from the existence of a particular institution have outweighed the attendant disadvantages. But does such an uncertain concept furnish a basis for a theory of reward proportioned to the degree of social service? Suppose that an exact quantitative esti-

12

mate of a non-computable social service could be formed and could be attributed to some particular business undertaking in which a fortune has been invested. Even then, it would not be possible to say what part of the estimated social service ought to be accredited to the owner of the wealth so invested. If, as has been contended, non-personal factors play an important part in the making of great fortunes, then a part of the benefit derived by the community at large from the existence of a particular fortune would have to be attributed to those non-personal factors, rather than to the ability of the owner of the fortune.[1]

It is sometimes said that a social service grows out of the existence of a fortune, in so far as that fortune represents capital employed in hiring laborers. Once more, how estimate the extent of that service? If, for instance, the laborers are employed under conditions inimical to life and health, or even if they are no better off than they were before, it is difficult to decide whether such employment can in any way be figured as a gain to them or to the community. But granting favorable conditions of work and a resultant gain, does the size of the fortune furnish even the

---

[1] As has been shown, there is no possibility of a sharp delimitation of the spheres of action of personal and non-personal factors.

roughest indication of the degree of social service growing out of the employment of labor? May not the small fortune, judged from such a point of view, be of much greater relative significance than the large fortune, since the latter usually represents a proportionately greater investment in purely acquisitive aids to gain-getting, such as franchises and special privileges of various sorts? What can be said for a great fortune made by land-speculations? By stock-gambling operations?

Not only is there no way of demonstrating any measurable connection between reward and social service, but it can be shown that the aggrandizement of the individual may take place without appreciable effect upon society, or, it may be, to its positive injury. So it is in the case of land investments. The buyer of real estate may shift possession from one lot to another with great profit to himself, although he may not have sought during his term of possession to improve in the least the condition of such properties. It is an open question whether John Jacob Astor hindered the development of the community rather more than he advanced it by his purchases of real estate. To be sure, he made improvements upon certain lots either directly or through the agency of his tenants. But it is doubtful whether the hotels and other buildings erected might not have been placed there even sooner by others; whether, given a change of ownership, land left unimproved might not have been ministering to definite public needs. In general, the case for withholding building lots from use is by no means clear. Because a piece of land may some day come into the heart of a business centre and be used as a site for a large office building, need by no means prevent its being employed to subserve certain present-day needs of the community. Indeed, so far as those present-day needs are legitimate, the owner who permits his land to remain unimproved performs a distinct social disservice.[2]

Moreover, take the case of the financier, who has only a secondary interest in the actual working arrangements of the organizations in which he has invested (and those working arrangements are, after all, the important thing for society). He is interested in them only in so far

---

[2]The possession of land may mean something more than a simple, passive holding of it, for the sake of its future increase in value. Its owner may put it to some use which subserves a definite public need, or he may perform a social service by withholding it from use for a certain period. In the case of farm, forest, and mineral lands, those owners who refrain from utilizing their holdings frequently accomplish a great public benefit by retarding the tendency to a too hasty development of natural resources. But here again, how establish a connection between the gain that may result to the individual and the value of the social service?

as they affect the value of his share holdings, and it may conceivably be to his advantage so to demoralize the mechanical organization as temporarily to depress the value of those shares. But apart from such questionable tactics, he may profit largely by judiciously shifting his investments from one field to another, without appreciable effect upon the industrial situation. He merely takes advantage of existing conditions which make for gain.

The evidence afforded by the fortune of Jay Gould excellently supports the contention that the amount of a man's gain bears no necessary relation to the degree of social service rendered, and, further, that such gain may even grow at the expense of the community.[3] When Gould left the Erie Railroad, he was richer by millions, but the Erie itself was one degree worse off than when he allied himself with it. In so far as his gains were the result of illegitimate practice, this statement has no great significance for economic theory; but in so far as they were obtained within

---

[3]"It would be very difficult to show that the nation as a whole is a dollar richer by the existence of Jay Gould, while he himself has become the richer by an amount estimated as aforesaid from the expansion of the city and the nation. He has simply absorbed what would have been made in spite of him, and what, if he had not interfered, would have been possessed by somebody else." From an editorial in the New York *Times*, December 3, 1892.

the limits of legal morality, such an assertion is of deep import. It means that the operator in stocks or other securities, by taking advantage of price fluctuations, may profit without the slightest reference to the material, technological, social facts of industry, or, it may be, as the result of socially injurious changes.

In his conduct of the Union Pacific, Gould certainly effected some actual improvements. For one thing, he extended the branch line system— an admitted good. But did he do it as economically, as prudently as might be? In point of fact, he seriously crippled the main line by some of the purchases made in his own interests. However, it would probably be fair to say that in this respect, the advantages outweighed the disadvantages. And so it goes with all the roads with which he was connected. No doubt certain tangible results were obtained, certain improvements made, but the question remains as to whether, under other auspices, those improvements might not have been a great deal more numerous, and effected with a much greater degree of economy. An answer to these queries may be conjectured, and it is not favorable to Gould. The fact that in nearly every instance these roads were bankrupt when he took them, were rehabilitated by him, saddled with vastly increased obligations,

and then allowed to lapse into bankruptcy once
again—all this does not favor the supposition of
economical and socially desirable management.

Again, take the case of the American Union
Telegraph Co., organized solely to levy blackmail
on the Western Union. Gould accomplished his
purpose of securing a combination of the two organizations, but the advantages which he as an
individual derived from his entry into the Western Union were obtained at a great social cost.
Four hundred and twenty-nine offices of the
American Union were closed following the consolidation; there had been a useless paralleling of
lines; Gould's victory spelt waste. No doubt,
once in control of the Western Union, his management was just as good as that of his prede-
cessors, since, happily, he believed in the Western
Union as an investment concern, and was, therefore, interested to maintain a high degree of
working efficiency.

What of the profits accruing to the "Standard
Oil" and "Morgan" men as the result of the extensive ramifications and interrelations of their
property holdings? Do they always represent a
social service? Or is it likely that technological
or other considerations making for increased social efficiency have been subordinated to a desire
to secure the gains incident to a concentration of

control over a wide field of trade and industry? An illustration may be drawn from the case of the United States Steel Corporation. All its constituent companies represented large combinations of capital, and were more or less industrially complete units in themselves. Viewed wholly from the industrial standpoint, therefore, the question might well have arisen as to whether a further unification might not prove so unwieldy as to offset any resultant economies. But to put all such considerations aside, the main purpose of the union was accomplished in that it prevented a war of the large financial interests, bringing together as it did the Morgan, Moore, Rockefeller, Carnegie, and Gates holdings. The Northern Securities Company is another illuminating example of a corporation organized purely and simply to secure a unification of the investment interests concerned, and to enjoy the profits incident to harmonious action.

The earlier combinations, such as those in steel, sugar, and petroleum, had come about in part, at least, as the result of industrial exigencies. At any rate, they certainly made for increased facilities of production within the limits of the industries in question. But it is difficult to see how certain present-day combinations can have any effect upon methods, processes, and economies of production, although such combinations may be highly profitable to the individuals in control of them by extending the scope of their influence, and adding to the size of their monopolistic gains.

It has been shown that there is no way of establishing a determinate relation between reward and personal ability, or reward and social service. What, then, can be said of the attempts of certain economists to combine the two ideas and to prove that "profits are the share or income of the entrepreneur for his skill in directing industry and in assuming the risks" and that "despite the complex influences they are determined by his contribution to industry, essentially as is the value of any skilled service."[4]   Is this any more than a dogmatic assertion, which is frequently

---

[4]Are the rewards of the successful enterpriser greater than he deserves?   How shall it be judged what he deserves?   The answer is in the form of a question, "Could society have the service without the reward?"   Society may be thought of as hiring the services of the efficient business man at the lowest price.   Does it wish the services of Cornelius Vanderbilt in organizing a great system of railroads, of Andrew Carnegie, of Pierpont Morgan?   What can it get them for?   It must appeal not only to their love of money but to their love of power.   Large services and large results can be bought only with large rewards."

Fetter, *Principles of Economics*, p. 377.

Would it be correct to infer from this that if the rewards of these men had been less, they would have done less?   Isn't it misleading to speak of "hiring" the services of these men, just as if the size of their returns were predestined, and could find expression in a stable contractual relation?   Even suppose it were necessary to guarantee them a fixed amount, would it be very illuminating to say that they deserve what they get because they insist upon having it?

contradicted by the facts. Professor Fetter himself, as a preliminary to the statements just quoted, discusses "anti-social or pseudo" profits, "chance" profits, and profits "due to a union of chance and choice."[5] He even says that "it still sometimes appears better to be born lucky than rich." Yet he concludes that "continuing profits arise from the continued exercise of superior judgment." Are, then, these chance elements so transient, unimportant, and "abnormal," that a valid theory of distribution can disregard them?

What, moreover, is the significance of the following statement, which, curiously enough, appears under the general caption that "incomes from legitimate enterprise and speculation correspond roughly to social service"? Professor Fetter admits that "in many ways fortunes appear to grow without social service, and sometimes with positive social harm." Russell Sage, the noted capitalist (who should know something of Wall Street), in speaking of the greatest of American corporations, said: "They dominate wherever they choose to go. They can make and unmake any property, no matter how vast. They can almost compel any man to sell out anything, at any price." Henry Clews, the well-known New York

---

[5] Fetter, *Principles of Economics*, pp. 289, 290.

banker, said of a certain group of financiers: "Their resources are so vast that they need only to concentrate on any given property in order to do with it what they please. . . . There is an utter absence of chance that is terrible to contemplate. This combination controls Wall Street almost absolutely. With such power and facilities it is easily conceivable that these men must make enormous sums on either side of the market."[6] Again, can a theory dismiss as an exception so salient a fact of our industrial development? Isn't the whole movement toward an extension of investment interests designed to minimize and to neutralize risk? It really seems as if risks of loss diminished with the growth in size of a man's income. Far from profits being due to superior skill in taking risks, profits usually increase as in the course of the general process of fortune development, there are fewer risks left to be assumed.

Professor Carver, in his book on the "Distribution of Wealth," has a category of profits, which he does not impute to the productivity of land, labor, or capital, but he gets it by confessing that his theory does not always hold in practice. The amounts paid for the hire of the several agents of

---

[6]Fetter, *Principles of Economics*, pp. 377, 378.

production are only "approximately" equal to their marginal products. "Of course, the owners of these factors of production will not knowingly take less than their marginal products, because that is what they are really worth. . . . But it is never known precisely what their marginal products are at any given time."[7] Profit is, then, resolved into the reward of risk-taking (which in Professor Carver's theory belongs logically under the head of wages) and the reward of superior bargaining. However, the share resulting from the business man's superior bargaining power produces nothing. In fact, a reward thus obtained has about it a suspicion of illegitimacy. It is a species of robbery, which, under more nearly ideal conditions, tends to disappear.[8] Thus Professor Carver is practically left with personal ability determining the value of a man's contribution to society (his social service), and hence the amount of his reward. But, he says, the amount which he can add to the social product is, on the principle of

---

[7] Carver, *The Distribution of Wealth,* Chap. VII, p. 260.

[8] J. B. Clark, *Distribution of Wealth,* Chap. XIX, p. 290, says: "Profit is the universal lure that makes the competition work and the ultimate goal of the whole movement is a no profit state." In other words, there is no room for a discussion of exceptional returns due to luck or chance in Professor Clark's productivity theory of distribution. Such returns must be reckoned transient or illegitimate, whenever they cannot be forced into the category of "regular" rewards assignable to the productivity of specific factors or agents.

marginal productivity, decreased as the number of business managers increases. That is, the man's actual ability is unchanged, his material contribution is unaltered, but his marginal (value) productivity, hence the size of his reward, is less. What, in reality, is this statement but a confession that rewards are not made solely on the "absolute" grounds of personal ability and social service, but are conditioned by various non-calculable circumstances?

Many economists who attempt to explain personal gain on the basis of ability, of social service, or of ability and social service in conjunction, either specifically state or else strongly imply that their theories furnish a justification of such gains. Suppose, however, that any one or all of these propositions could be established. Wherein would lie the "justification" of the existence of gains? The proof would have an ethical validity only in so far as it coincided with one's metaphysical predilections. Assume, for instance, that a man's ability was so great that none could compete with him, or that he performed an incalculably valuable social service. Would he be "justified" in engrossing the earth? Would society, in either case, meekly allow all its possessions to remain at his disposal? Certainly not; it would feel under no metaphysical compulsion to permit such a consummation, and it would, if need were, find means to prevent it.

To talk, then, of justifying the winnings of the man of great fortune is idle. He stands or falls, as this or that view of social expediency prevails. At present, the general belief seems to be, that, under the existing economic system, social needs are fairly well met, and the majority of the people receive a reward just about sufficient to make them exert their full powers toward the satisfaction of those needs. It is further assumed that this approximation to the socially desirable can only be secured by permitting a high degree of liberty of action and freedom of acquisition to all members of the social group. If, however, certain men or groups of men, while operating within the existing legal limitations, should succeed in securing a large share of the property of the community with all the attendant influence that ownership implies, opinion regarding the socially desirable nature of present economic arrangements might undergo a transformation. If such cases became sufficiently numerous and insistent, there might arise a demand for regulative changes. It would then be for the community to decide upon the necessity, scope, and character of the proposed new measures. And its decision should properly be made on the broad basis of public policy. On such ground, purely economic facts and the preconceptions of economic science will secure recognition, to be sure, but only to the extent that they have a direct bearing upon the wider question of the general public welfare.

Big Business

Economic Power in a Free Society

An Arno Press Collection

La Follette, Robert Marion, editor. **The Making of America:** Industry and Finance. 1905

Lilienthal, David E. **Big Business:** A New Era. 1952

Lippincott, Isaac. **A History of Manufactures in the Ohio Valley to the Year 1860.** 1914

Lloyd, Henry Demarest. **Lords of Industry.** 1910

McConnell, Donald. **Economic Virtues in the United States.** 1930

Mellon, Andrew W. **Taxation:** The People's Business. 1924

Meyer, Balthasar Henry. **Railway Legislation in the United States.** 1909

Mills, James D. **The Art of Money Making.** 1872

Montague, Gilbert Holland. **The Rise and Progress of the Standard Oil Company.** 1904

Mosely Industrial Commission. **Reports of the Delegates of the Mosely Industrial Commission to the United States of America, Oct.-Dec., 1902.** 1903

Orth, Samuel P., compiler. **Readings on the Relation of Government to Property and Industry.** 1915

Patten, Simon N[elson]. **The Economic Basis of Protection.** 1890

Peto, Sir S[amuel] Morton. **Resources and Prospects of America.** 1866

Ripley, William Z[ebina]. **Main Street and Wall Street.** 1929

Ripley, William Z[ebina]. **Railroads:** Rates and Regulation. 1912

Rockefeller, John D. **Random Reminiscences of Men and Events.** 1909

Seager, Henry R. and Charles A. Gulick, Jr. **Trust and Corporation Problems.** 1929

Taeusch, Carl F. **Policy and Ethics in Business.** 1931

Taylor, Albion Guilford. **Labor Policies of the National Association of Manufacturers.** 1928

Vanderlip, Frank A. **Business and Education.** 1907

Van Hise, Charles R. **Concentration and Control:** A Solution of the Trust Problem in the United States. 1912

The Wealthy Citizens of New York. 1973

White, Bouck. **The Book of Daniel Drew.** 1910

Wile, Frederic William, editor. **A Century of Industrial Progress.** 1928

Wilgus, Horace L. **A Study of the United States Steel Corporation in Its Industrial and Legal Aspects.** 1901

[Youmans, Edward L., compiler] **Herbert Spencer on the Americans.** 1883

Youngman, Anna. **The Economic Causes of Great Fortunes.** 1909